Tyler Burgess

EUGENE and SPRINGFIELD TOWNSCAPE WALKS

50 walks
240 miles

2nd edition

Walk with Me → Tyler E. Burgess

Published by:
Walk With ME
1430 Willamette St. #579
Eugene, OR 97401
Printed in the USA.
Walk-With-Me.com

These are unique routes I
designed as I walked them,
with exceptions of designated
trails. Construction and
business changes can alter
the routes.

What is a Townscape Walk?

"For a city is a dramatic event
in the environment." by
George Cullen, "Townscape", 1961.

What makes a townscape walk dramatic?
"The line of Life." Why is this city here?
Look for clues in historic areas.

"The Grandoise Vista." It links you, in the
foreground, to the remote view,
Thus producing a sense of power,
or omnipresence.

"Mystery of the Emerging View."
What is around the corner,
over the hill, down the path?

"The Silhouette." With a curve, a steeple, the
buildings soar up to catch the
sky, netting it as the
butterfly net catches it's prey.

"Seeing in detail." A window, fences, a symbol,
an arch, a bridge, a garden.
Outdoor rooms: Porches, benches,
and gazebos create seclusion or
invite social activity.

INTRODUCTION

These walking routes are mostly an accumulation of walks I led as a walking instructor at the U. of Oregon and Lane Community College.

Many thanks to the hundreds of people who walked with me. You made all walks more fun.

My walking tips

1. Start slowly, go easy. Start with 10 to 20 minute walks. Add 5 minutes to daily walks every 2 weeks. Walk by minutes, not miles.

2. Goal: Walk one hour a day for the rest of your life.

3. Wear good walking or running shoes. Get good gear and go outside every day.

4. Stretch afterwards.
   Stretch up, then down.
   and Thigh Stretch. Five times. Every day.

How to Use This Book

- <u>Start/finish point</u>.
  For shorter options, some
  maps have more than one
  start point. Also, there
  short cuts on most maps.

<u>Elevation gain</u>: Number
of feet going up.

- <u>Bus</u>: Routes are marked
on the maps.
see www.ltd.org. LTD

<u>Restrooms</u>
 <u>Open year round</u> at
  Alton Baker Park
  Amazon Parkway and 24th Ave.
 <u>Open seasonally</u> (April to Oct.)
  Monroe Park
  Tugman Park
 <u>Springfield</u>
  Dorris Ranch
  Mill Race Trailheads
  Thurston Hills Trail

Legend
.... shorter route
〜〜 hill
T = toilet P = parking
food = grocery, market, or cafe. Do buy
        something if you use facilities.

mi. = mileage
R = right. L = left.
elevation = feet of ascent

Table of Contents

EUGENE

1. Golden Gardens Pond.
      miles: 1 to 4, flat.
      p.12

2. Ashley Estates.
      miles: 1 to 2, flat.
      p.14

3. Christmas Lights. 1.5 mi. flat.
      p.15

4. Honeywood Hop.
      miles: 2, 3.2, 4.2, flat.
      p.16

5. Pretty Ponds.
      miles: 3, 5.4, 6.7, 8.7. flat
      p.18

Starting at Alton Baker Park

6. Butte to Bakery.
      miles: 2.5, 3.5, 400 ft. elev.
      p.20

7. Historic Homes.
      miles: 2, 3.2, 4.7, flat
      p.22

8. Pre's Rock. 300 ft. elevation.
      miles: 2.5, 4.5, 6.5.
      p.24

9. Spyglass.
      miles: 1.2, 4.2, 6.2. 92 ft. elev.
      p.26

10. Gillespie Butte.
      miles: 1, 3, 6. 114 ft. elevation.
      p.28

11. River Bike Path.
      miles: up to 12, flat.
      p.30

12. Pre's Trail
      miles: 4. flat. bark trails.
      p.32

EUGENE

13. Rose Garden Route.
miles: 4, 6. flat.   p. 34

14. Sweet Life Loop.
miles: 1.5, 2.5, 4. flat.   p. 36

15. Cornucopia.
miles: 1, 2, 3.1. flat.   p. 38

16. Fern Ridge Path Bike.
miles: 7 mi. one way. flat.   p. 40

17. Friendly Street Loop.
miles: 3.5, 4, 5.5. 434 ft. elev. p. 42

18. Hawkin's Haunts.
miles: 2, 3.6, 5.3. 347 ft. elev. p. 44

19. UO Campus Big Trees.
miles: 1.5, 3. flat.   p. 46

20. Hendricks Park, Ribbon Trail.
miles: 3, hilly.   p. 48

21.. Hendricks Park, Fire Break Road.
miles: 2.5, hilly.   p. 50

22. Hendricks Park, Floral Hill.
miles: 3.5. hilly.   p. 52

23. Ridgeline Trail, hilly.
miles: 1. Many options.   p. 54

24. Ridgeline Trail, Long Loop,
miles: 10.3 mi. hilly.   p. 56

25. Ridgeline: Cold Spring, 1.5 mi.   p. 58

26. Ridgeline: Spencer Butte.
three ways up   p. 59

EUGENE

(Starting at Amazon Pkwy. and 24th Ave.)

27. Beautiful Alley
               miles: 1.7, 3. 110 ft. elev.   p.60

28. City Views, up to 709 ft. elev.
               miles: 2.3, 3.6, 7.7, 9.8   p.62

29. Edgewood Trails 1
               miles: 6.4 , 498 ft. elev. p.64

30. Emerald Hill
               miles: 1.5, 2.5 116 ft. elev. p.66

31. Elk Street.
               miles: 4. 5.   p.68

32. Fairmount Trail, 227 ft. elev.
               miles: 2, 2.5, 4.   p.70

33. Four Creeks, 540 ft. elev.
               miles: 2, 2.5, 3.5, 7.   p.72

34. Mansions and Meadows.
               miles: 4.4, 7, 9. Hilly.   p.74

35. Lafferty Park.
               miles: 5.5.   p.76

36. Adidas-Rexius Trail
               miles: 5.5 , flat, bark.   p.78

37. Exploring Edgewood Trails.
               mile: 1 on asphalt path. p.80

38. Edgewood Trails 2.
               miles: 6.4 498 ft. elev.   p.82

39. LCC Labrynith and Trails
               miles: 2.7   p.84

EUGENE MAP

Map not to exact scale.

W N E S

1 ← Golden Gardens Park

Beltline

Owosso

Copping

River Bike Path

River Road

Hillcrest

River Path

Good Pasture

Delta Hwy

Willagillespie

Delta Bridge

Path

Delta Hwy.

Meadow View

2 Ayres

4 Honeywood

Lakeview

3

5 Green Acres

Gilham

Crescent

Mckenzie

Beltline

To I-5 Springfield →

Coburg

10 Debrick

Clinton

Cal Young

Gillespie Butte

Oakway

5 Valley River Mall

Greenway

Willamette

River Path

13 Rose Garden

Country Club Rd

105-126

River Playarea

105-126 to I-5

MLK Blvd

6 to 12

Autzen Football Stadium

Alton Baker Park

Chambers

Monroe St.

Jefferson

Washington

2nd

High

River Path

Amtrak Train

126-99 6th

7th

River Path

Seneca

10th

11th

14

Down town

Bus

Franklin

11th

To I-5 Springfield →

Hospital

13th

19

15th

Path

15 St.

18 Buck

W. 18th

Fern

Ridge Path

Polk

16 17

15 St.

Chamelton

17th

18th

15

18th

Pearl

18th

UO

University St.

Agate

track

0

20, 21, 22 Hendricks Park

Jefferson

Monroe

Friendly

Willamette St.

Amazon

27 to 36

24th Av.

27th Av.

28th Av.

29th

Hilyard

30th Av. to LCC to I-5

39

39th

Donald

40th

40th

38

Brae Burn

37

46th

Willamette

Fox Hollow

W. Amazon Pkwy

Center

52nd

26 to Spencer Butte Park

23 to 26

Martin

to Ridgeline trail

9

Springfield

40. By-Gully Path.
        miles: 5.25., flat.   p.86

41. Kelly Butte..
        miles: 2 flat, 3.5. 180 ft. elev.   p.88

42. Washburne Historic District.
        miles: 1.2, 2.3, 3.5   flat.   p.90

43. Willamette Heights Park.
        miles: 2, big hill.   p.92

44. Dorris Ranch
        miles: 1.5 to 4, flat.   p.94

45. Mill Race Path-Clearwater Park.
Middle Fork Path.
        miles: 1 to 5. flat.   p.96

46. Hayden Bridge Way.
        miles: 2.4, 3.4. flat.   p.98

47. River Bend River Trail.
        mile: 2.5. flat.   p.100

48. Thurston H.S. to Ivy St.
    miles: 2.8 or 5.   p.102

49. Mountaingate Trails.
        miles: 4.5, 400 ft. elev.   p.104

50. Thurston Hills
        miles: 1.9, one way. Hill.   p.106

    Walker's Diary   p.107
    About the Author   p.110

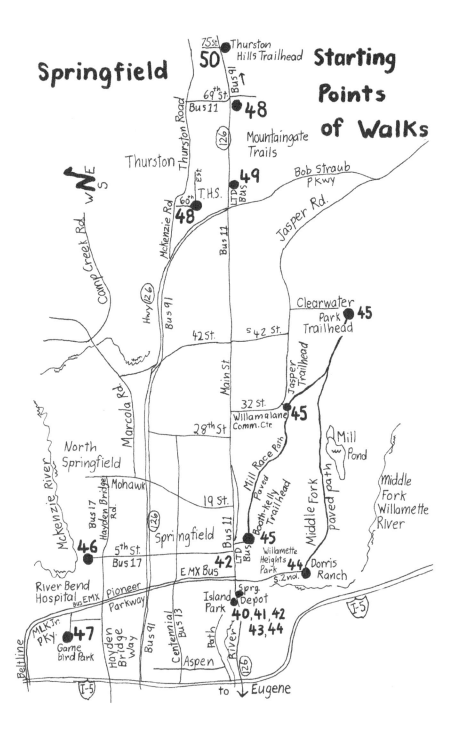

Springfield

Starting Points of Walks

75 st.
50
Thurston Hills Trailhead

Bus 91

69th St.
Bus 11
48

Thurston Road
126

Mountaingate Trails

Bob Straub Pkwy

Thurston

W N E S

61st.
T.H.S.
49
LTD Bus

Jasper Rd.

McKenzie Rd.
60th
48

Camp Creek Rd.

Bus 11

Hwy 126

Bus 91

Clearwater Park Trailhead
45

42 St.
S 42 St.

Jasper Trailhead

Main St.

32 St.
Willamalane Comm. Ctr.
45

Marcola Rd.

North Springfield

28th St.

Mill Race Path

Mill Pond

Middle Fork Willamette River

McKenzie River

Mohawk

19 St.

Paved Booth-Kelly Trailhead
45

Middle Fork

paved path

Hayden Bridge Rd.

126

Springfield

Bus 11

Willamette Heights Park
44
Dorris Ranch

Bus 17

5th St.
Bus 17

LTD Bus

42

River Bend Hospital

Pioneer Parkway

E MX Bus

S. 2nd.

Bus EMX

Sprg. Depot

MLK Jr. Pky.
47
Game bird Park

Hayden Bridge Way

Bus 91

Centennial Bus 13

Island Park

River Path

40, 41, 42
43, 44

Beltline

I-5

Aspen

126

I-5

to ↓ Eugene

GOLDEN GARDENS PARK

Distance : 1 to 4 miles. Flat.
Start/finish: Golden Gardens St. and Jessen Dr.

Walk into park. Straight on to
bark path, circle back to start.

Cross Jessen Dr. **R** on sidewalk.
L on Devos St., one block.
R on path after 2212 Devos St.
Across the park, on the path.
Jog **R** at street to stay on path.

R at end, on Trevon St.
L at end Terry St.
R on Coetivy.
Cross next street.

Jog **L** and **R** by 2202 to path.
L on Dakota, **R** across park.
R at street (Wisconsin).

L on Cody Ave. **R** on Ohio St.
R on path back to start.
(This path to be completed
in fall 2018. Or return as you
came.)

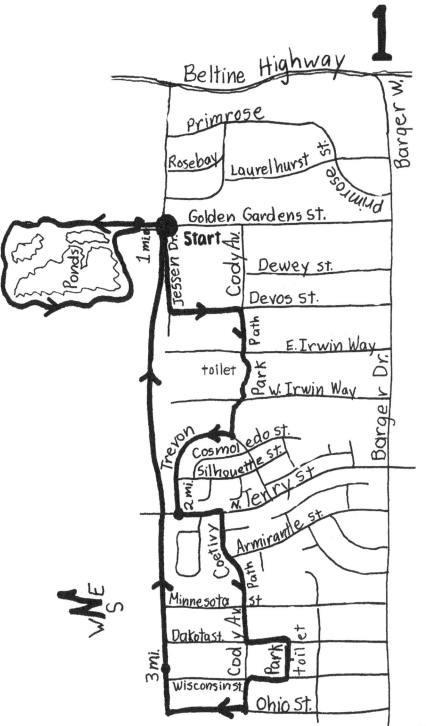

1

2 ASHLEY ESTATES

Start/finish: Ashley Estates, off Ayres Rd.
on Meadow View Way.
Distance: 1 mi. or 2 mi. Flat.

Walk down Meadow View Way.
R at end, on Mirror Pond Way.
(for 1 mi. option. **R** on Quail Meadow Way.

R on Gilham.
R on Crimson Av.

L on Quail Meadows.
R at next corner, River Pointe Dr.
R on Ayres, back to finish.

CHRISTMAS LIGHTS 3

or Any Time

Distance: 1.5 mi. flat.

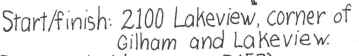

Start/finish: 2100 Lakeview, corner of
Gilham and Lakeview.

R on Northridge (house 3153).
L on Elkhorn. **R** on Lakeview.
R on Marie Ln. **R** on Sarah Ln.

L on Crescent Dr. **L** on Cheryl.
L into Pine Grove cul de sac,
then straight on Pine Grove.

L on Parkvieview Dr, 1 block.
L on Lakeview.

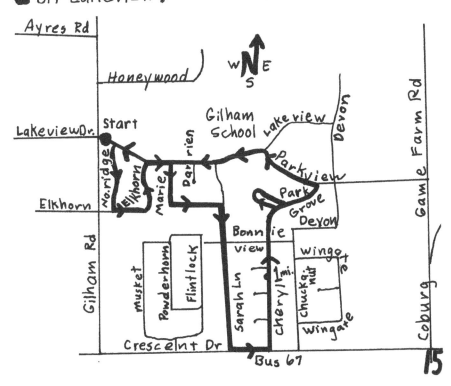

HONEYWOOD HOP

Distance: 2mi., 3.2 mi., 4.2 miles. flat.
Start/finish: On Honeywood St. at Gilham Rd.

Walk on Honeywood St. curves left.
R on Wester St. **R** on Downing St.
L on Dale St. **R** on Devon Av.
      R on Parkview St.

(for 2 mi. option. Stay on Parkview.
R on Gilham St. to Honeywood.)

L at next corner, to Park Grove.
Continue around cul de sac, then
R at 2318 Park Grove.

a loop
{
L on Bonnie View, **R** on Chuckanut.
L on Wingate. **R** on Chuckanut.
L on Bonnie View, onto path
}

R at end, to Carriage, to Musket, } a
  to Flintlock. **R** after #2963, to path. } loop
L after path. **L** at end, on Lakeview.

(for 3.2 mi. option, **R** on Gilham.
R on Honeywood to finish.)

Cross Gilham on Lakeview Dr.
Curve to Metolius.

L on Wolf Meadows Ln.
R on Lakeview.
L on Gilham.
R on Honeywood to finish.

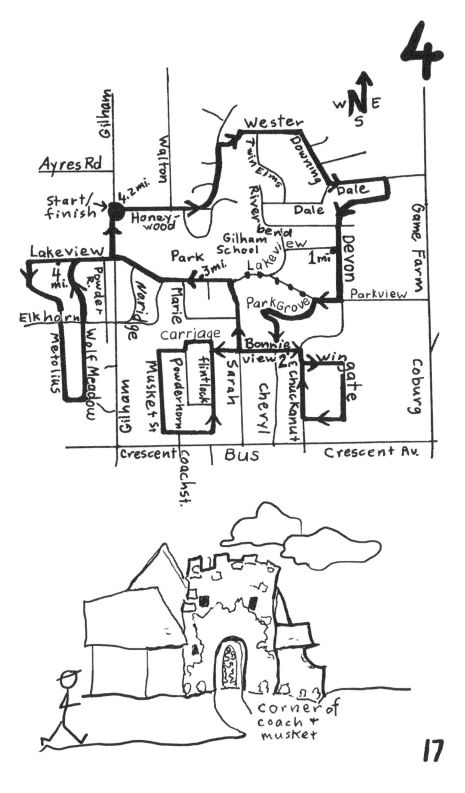

4

W **N** E
S

Wester

Ayres Rd

Gilham

Walton

Twin Elms

Downing

Dale

Dale

Game Farm

4.2 mi.

Start/
finish

Honey-
wood

Riverbend

Gilham
School

Lakeview

Devon

1 mi

Lakeview

Park

.3mi.

Lakeview

Powder R.

4
mi.

Maridge

Marie

ParkGrove

Parkview

Coburg

Elkhorn

Metolius

Wolf Meadow

carriage

Bonnie
view 2

wingate

Flintlock

Sarah

cheryl

E Chuckanut

Musket St

Powderhorn

Gilham

Crescent

Bus

coach st.

Crescent Av.

corner of
coach +
musket

17

PRETTY PONDS

Distance: 5.4mi, *6.7mi, or 8.5 miles. Flat.
Start/finish: Behind Valley River Mall
along river

Face river, go **R** to end.
Cross Delta. Highway. Go **L**.
R on Stapp. **L** on Delta Pines.
R on Ayres. **R** on Gilham.

R on Lakeview, curves to go
R on Gilham. **R** on Holly.
Cross Norakenzie. Go **L**eft.

R on Linda, go straight. *
L on Tabor. **L** on Larkspur.
R on Montrey. **R** on Norakenzie

R on Bond. **L** on Fir Acres.
Cross Cal Young.
Straight to Debrick.

R on Rio Glen, to R. Hood Dr. Over Delta Bridge.
Straight, use the crosswalk, **L** on path along river.

For 5.4 mile

After Owosso bridge, **R** on paved path
L at fork. **L** at street, Goodp. Loop.
L on Goodpasture Is. Rd.

Over Delta Hwy. on overpass. At light,
R across Goodpasture Is. Rd. to path
on the Right. Follow path.
R on Willagillespie. **R** on R. Hood st.
L on bike path.

18

For 6.7 miles: Walk on Green Acres.
R on Nora kenzie. See ✳

5

Ayres Rd.
Lake ridge
Lake shore
4mi
Honey-wood
Lakeview
W N E S
Delta Hwy
Delta pines
Stapp Dr.
3mi.
stores
Metolius
Wolf Meadow
Powder
Elkhorn
mi. Gilham
Path
Beltline Hwy
Food
6.7 mi.
Green Acres
Balboa
Tulip
Balboa
5
Holly
Acacia
Norakenzie
Holly
.54 mi option
foot bridge
Owosso
2mi
Lakes
Loop
River
Walk Loop
Goodpasture
wal-Mart
Beltline Hwy
Willona
Marist High School
mi.6
Linda
Ingle wood
Flintridge
Brewer
Corum
Linnea
Goodpasture Is Rd.
Jeppsen
Minda Dr.
1mi
Bike Path
Willamette River
Delta Hwy
Goodpasture Is Rd.
Tabor
Larkspur
monterey
Bond
7mi.
Fir Acres
Dari-Mart
Cal Young Rd.
Bachlund
Robin Hood
Rio Glen
Debrick
Brickley
Hammock
Seaglass
Clinton
Valley Butte
Crenshaw
Gillespie Butte cemetery
Ponds
Goodpasture Is Rd.
Valley River Dr.
Start/finish 8.5mi
Valley River Mall
T/P Bus
Bike Path
Valley River Wy
VRI
River Road Bus 51,52,55
Bike Path
Fir
Jacobs Park Bridge
Road
River W

19

BUTTE TO BAKERY

Distance: 2.5 mi. or 3.5 mi. Elevation 400ft.

Start/finish: Alton Baker Park. Walk to the river, over the foot bridge.

R after bridge.
L under car bridge. Quick
L off main path.
R at street, 2nd Av.

R on High St. Across crosswalk,
Up on the bark path. Take any
trail to the top. Continue to the
flagpole. From the flagpole, go
30 paces west to steep trail on
left.

Follow trail across the road.
Go **L** 30 paces. **R** down trail.
L around Victorian house.
Exit on driveway.

For 2.5 mi. option, go straight to
High St. **L** on High St. **R** on 2nd to park

R at street, Pearl St.
L on 11th Av. **L** on Hilyard St.
to the bike path.
L on main path.
L up path to bridge.
R Over bridge to park.

20

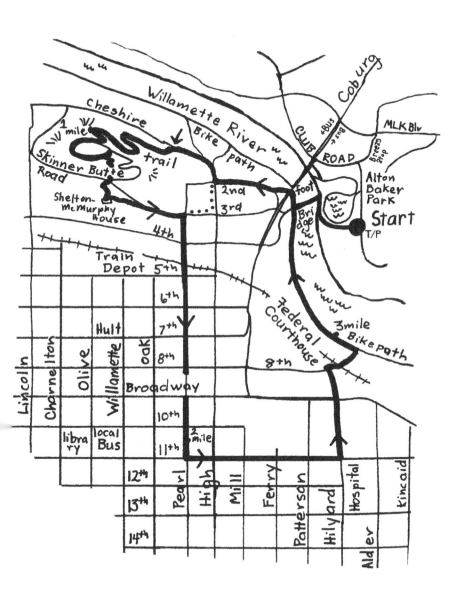

Western Trillium
in spring

HISTORIC HOMES

Distance: 2 mi., 3.2 mi., 4.7 mi. Flat.
Start/finish: Alton Baker Park.

Walk to the river. Go over the
arched foot bridge.
L after bridge.
L through big plaza.
R on bike path.

1883

W.H. ABRAHAMS' CIDER
Factory and FRUIT DRYER
(602 8ᵗʰ) a detour

R to path at to Hilyard sign.
L at street, to Hilyard.
      (for 2 mi., return to park)

170 E. 12 Av.
oldest house.

R on 11ᵗʰ Av., one block.
L Patterson St., one block.
R on 12ᵗʰ

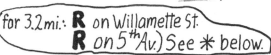

for 3.2 mi.: **R** on Willamette St.
     R on 5ᵗʰ Av.) See ✳ below.

L on Washington St.
Cross 13ᵗʰ Av. Go **R**.
R on Monroe St. **R** on 5ᵗʰ Av.
✳ **L** on High St. **L** in to alley after 4ᵗʰ Av.

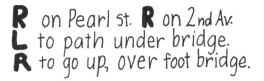

R on Pearl St. **R** on 2nd Av.
L to path under bridge.
R to go up, over foot bridge.

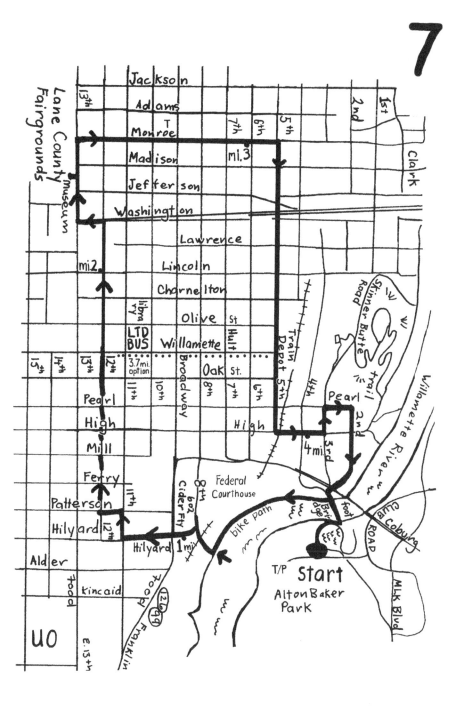

PRE'S ROCK

Distance: 2.5 mi., 4.5 mi or 6.5 mi. Elev. 300 ft.
      (For 2.5 mi.– Start at 15th and Agate St.)
Start/finish: Alton Baker Park

L on bike path along river.
After two miles, **R** over
foot bridge, Knickerbocker.
L at traffic light, onto Walnut.

(for 4.5 mi. **R** on 15th Av. See ***** below.)

L on 15th Av. **R** on Fairmount.
L on Birch St. **R** on Skyline St. (PRE'S ROCK) →

At parking lot, **R** past restrooms.
Take paths through park down
to street, Summit. **R** on Summit,
stay on path along Summit.

R on Fairmount.
L on 15th Av.

*R on Agate St.
L before footbridge on path.
L in big plaza.
R at street. Over bridge to park.

Skinner Butte   Gillespie Butte

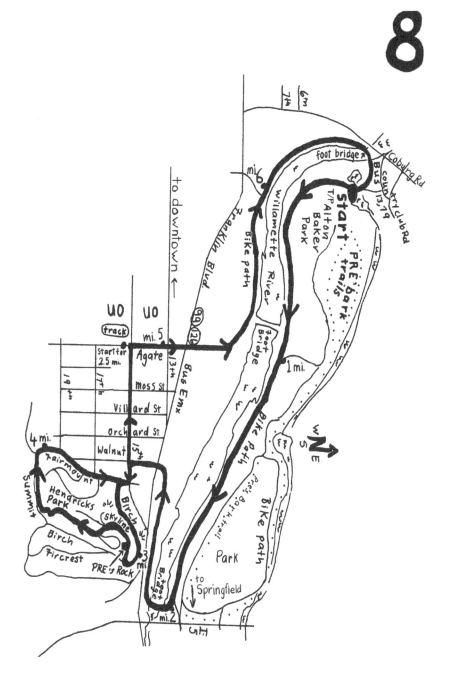

8

SPYGLASS

Distance:* 1.2 mi: Start at Spyglass and Cal Young.
4.2 mi: Start at Oakway Mall.
6.2 mi.: Start at Alton Baker Park.
Elevation gain: 92 ft.

In Alton Baker Park, walk past
the big foot bridge. Go up the
ramp to the car bridge.

R on bridge.
L at Oakway, before Mall.
Cross Oakway. **R**, to walk on
left side of Oakway Rd.

L on Eastwood Ln. **R** on Fairway Lp.
L on Fairoaks Dr. **L** on Oakway Rd.

L on St. Andrew's Dr. **L** on Oakway.
L on Law Ln. to end. **R** on Street.
L on Cal Young Rd.

L on sidewalk. <u>Before</u> traffic light.

R at street, Spyglass. (For 1.2 mi, start here.)*

L at corner, loop back to sidewalk.
R on Cal Young.
R on Oakway Rd, back to park.
→ or return the way you came.

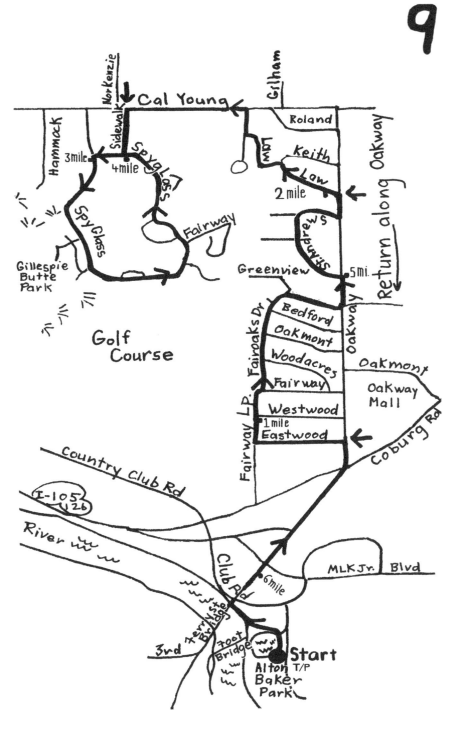

9

GILLESPIE BUTTE

Distance: 6 miles, 114 ft. elevation
start/finish: Alton Baker Park

Walk to the river, go **R**.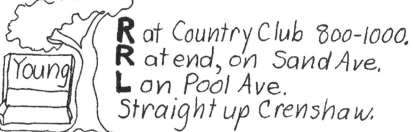
Under car bridge.
R at first fork.
Straight onto Country Club Rd.
Cross at a crosswalk. Continue.

R at Country Club 800-1000.
R R at end, on Sand Ave.
L on Pool Ave.
Straight up Crenshaw.

At hilltop, **R** into cemetery
Explore to end. **R**eturn to road.
R downhill.

R on Debrick Rd.
L on Rio Glen Dr.
Cross Willagillespie Rd.
     on to Robin Hood Ave.
Over the bridge.
Straight to the river.
L on Path, to the Park.

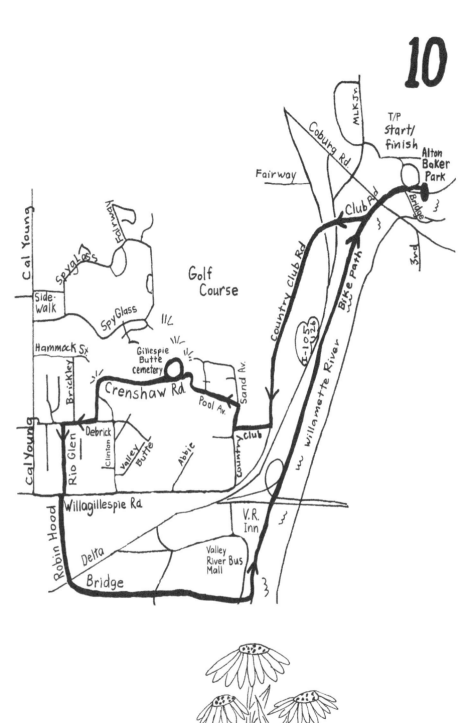

T/P
Start/
finish

Alton
Baker
Park

Coburg Rd

MLK Jr.

Fairway

Club Rd

Bridge

3rd

Cal Young

Fairway

SpyGlass

Golf
Course

Country Club Rd

I-105
126

Bike Path

Willamette River

Side-
walk

Spy Glass

711

Hammack St

Gillespie
Butte
cemetery

Sand Av.

Crenshaw Rd.

Brickley

Pool Av.

Debrick

Rio Glen

Clinton

Valley
Butte

Abbie

Country Club

Cal Young

Willagillespie Rd.

V.R.
Inn

Robin Hood

Delta

Valley
River Bus
Mall

Bridge

Willamette River
Bike Path

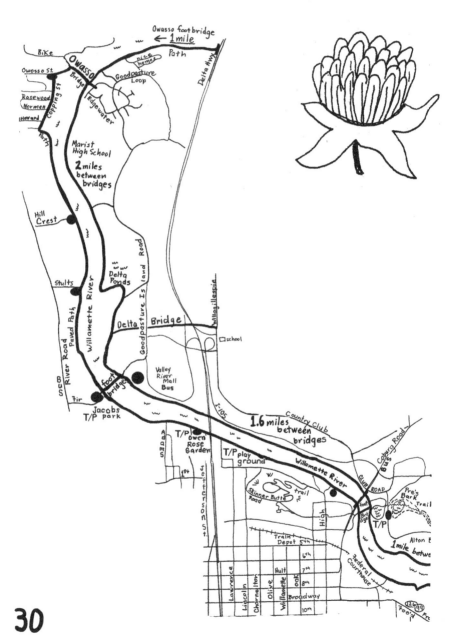

This is a flat, paved path along the river. **11**
See map for distances between bridges.
Quarter mile markers are embedded in path.
Restrooms: Alton Baker Park
           Rose Garden
           Skinner Butte Play Area
A dog park is opposite Autzen Stadium.

Bike Path Etiquette

Walk, or ride, on the right side.
Keep two abreast, to let people pass.
If cycling, announce yourself when
    passing, "on your left." <u>Loudly</u>.

Dogs must be leashed.
    It is the law.
    Scoop dog poop.
Use a light when it is dark.
Nod, smile, say hello to everyone.
    This is Eugene!

Bus: Valley River Mall. Find the
    bike path along the river.

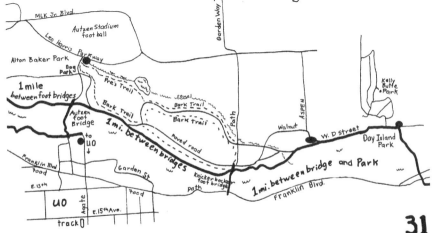

PRE'S TRAIL

Distance: up to 4 miles. Flat. <u>Bark trail</u>.
Start/finish: Alton Baker Park.

Find the large information board,
above the parking lot on the left of
the entrance.

Follow the trail behind the
board; about Steve Prefontaine.
L at the first fork.
Straight past the large
iron sculpture.

R over the bridge,
opposite the HUGE stadium.
L after the bridge.

L at fork, around the pond,
along the canal.
R before the overhead
bridge. Stay on trail.
R on trail along river.

L at pond.
After the pond, **L** on trail.
L at end. Veer **L** back
to the start.

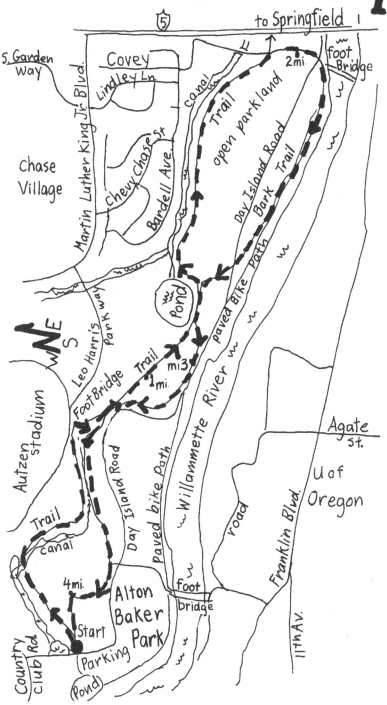

to Springfield

5

S. Garden way

Covey

Lindley Ln.

foot Bridge

2 mi.

Chase Village

Martin Luther King Jr. Blvd.

Chevy Chase St.

Bardell Ave.

canal

Trail

open parkland

Day Island Road

Bark Trail

Pond

paved Bike Path

Leo Harris Parkway

Foot Bridge

Trail

mi 3

¼ mi.

Willamette River

N E S W

Autzen Stadium

Trail

canal

Day Island Road

Paved bike path

Agate St.

U of Oregon

road

Franklin Blvd.

11th Av.

4 mi.

Alton Baker Park

foot bridge

Country Club Rd.

Start

Parking

Pond

ROSE GARDEN ROUTE

Distance: 4 mi. or 6 mi. Flat.

Start/finish: Owen Rose Garden, at north end
of Jefferson St.
From the parking lot, walk through
garden to bike path.
R on bike path 1¼ mi.

After the big plaza,
R on path to Hilyard St.
Cross railroad tracks.
L on street, Hilyard St.
R on 11ᵗʰ Av. for one block.
Cross Patterson St. Go **L**.
R on 15ᵗʰ Av.

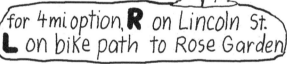

for 4 mi. option, **R** on Lincoln St.
L on bike path to Rose Garden

Where 15ᵗʰ Av. ends, continue
on to Fern Ridge Bike Path.
R on Polk St.
R on 4ᵗʰ Av.
L on Jefferson St.
to Rose Garden.

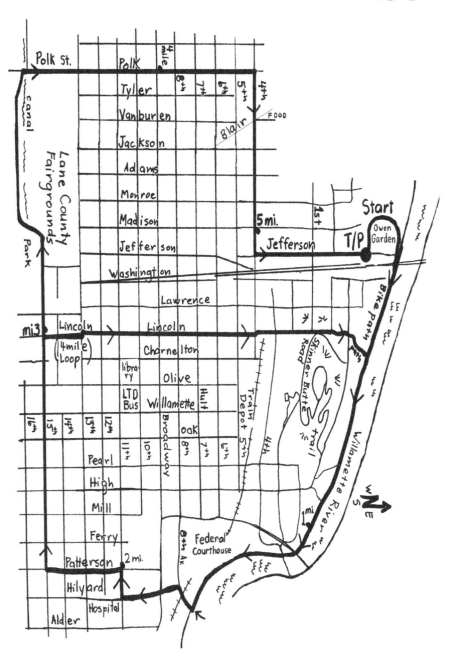

13

SWEET LIFE LOOP

Distance: 15 mi., 2.5 mi., or 4 mi. Flat

Start/finish: Monroe Park, at
              W. Broadway and 10th Av.

Facing the park,
R on W. Broadway.
L on Almaden St.
L on 10th Av.

755
Monroe

SWEET LIFE
PATISSERIE

For 1.5 mi. **L** on Monroe St.
one block back to park.

L on Olive St. one block.
L on W. Broadway St.

For 2.5 mi. stay on W. Broadway
to the park.

R on Madison st. into
   4-J parking lot.
L one block in lot.
L at first exit onto Monroe.
Follow to Monroe Park.

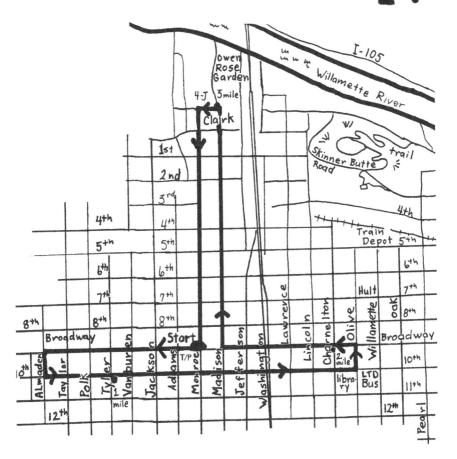

14

CORNUCOPIA

Distance: 1mi., 2 mi. (start at 16th and Friendly St.)
   3 mi. Flat.

Start/finish: W.17th Av. and Charnelton St.
Facing the park, walk down
Charnelton, one block.
L on W 16th Av. **R** on Lawrence.
L on W 15th Av. onto Fern Ridge Path.

1870
home,
barn

(for 1 mi, **L** off the paved path to
a gravel path, before Friendly St.
See ✳ below for directions.)

L over first foot bridge.
L after bridge on bark trail.
Walk the bark path looping
beyond the exercise stations.

   Walk toward the tennis courts,
   on to W 20th Av. Continue straight.

L on Friendly St.
R on Fern Ridge Path.
Straight to gravel path to W. 16th Av.

✳**R** on Washington St. one block.
   L on W. 17th Av. to park.

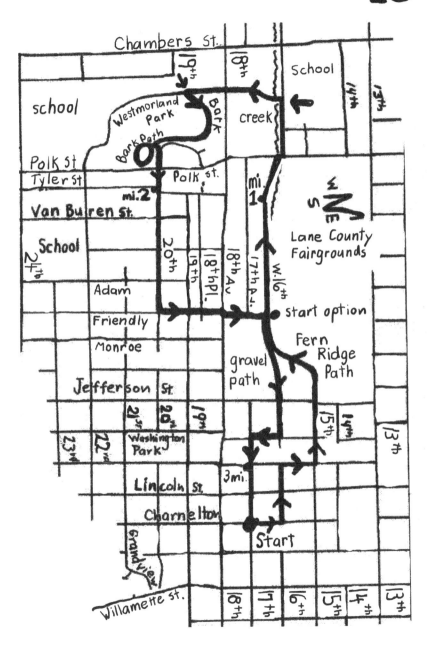

15

FERN RIDGE BIKE PATH

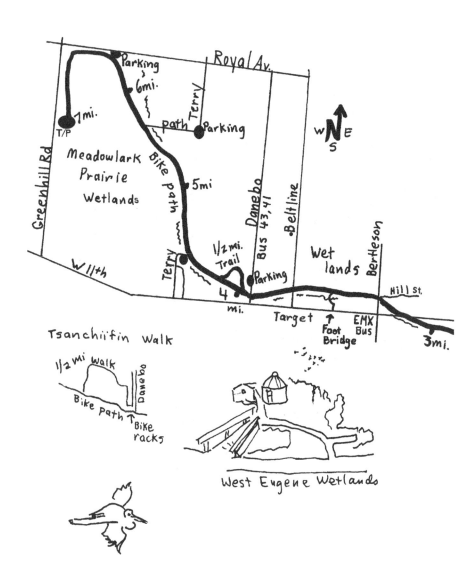

Royal Av.

Parking 6mi.

path Terry Parking

1mi.
T/P

Greenhill Rd

Meadowlark Prairie Wetlands

Bike path

5mi

Danebo Bus 43,41

Beltline

W 11th

Terry

1/2 mi. Trail

Parking

Wet lands

Berteson

Hill St.

4 mi.

Target

Foot Bridge

EMX Bus

3mi.

W N E S

Tsanchiifin Walk

1/2 mi walk

Bike Path

Danebo

Bike racks

West Eugene Wetlands

16

FERN RIDGE BIKE PATH

Distance: 7 miles from W.15ᵗʰ Av. and
Jefferson St. Flat, paved

Access streets for shorter options:
• Polk St. • Oak Patch • Acorn Park St.
• Bertleson and Hill st. • Danebo at Wetland Office.
• Terry St. off W.11ᵗʰ Av. and Royal Av.
• Royal Av. • Greenhill Rd.
Bus: EMX

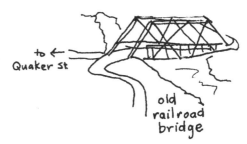

to ←
Quaker St

old
railroad
bridge

FRIENDLY St. LOOP

Distance: 3.5 mi., 4 mi or 5.5 miles
Elevation gain: 434 ft.

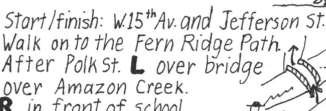

Start/finish: W.15th Av. and Jefferson St.
Walk on to the Fern Ridge Path.
After Polk St. **L** over bridge
over Amazon Creek.
R in front of school.
L at street. Filmore. St.

For 3.5 mi., **L** at Almaden St.
L on W.28th Av. **L** on Tyler St.
R on 27th. **L** on Friendly St.
R on bike path.

For 4 mi., **R** on W.28th Av. **L** on Chambers St.
L on Arendale st., Follow directions at ✳

J·TEA

R on W.28th Av. **L** on City View St.
L on W.29th Av. Curves to Mckendrick.
L on Karyl Av. Cross Street, Chambers.
R to corner. **L** on Arendale Ln.
✳ At end, veer **R** to foot path.

Cross street, Mclean. Go **L**.
R on Ingalls. Straight to Tiara.

L on Adams St. **R** on W.28th Av.
L on Friendly St.
R on Fern Ridge Path.

white oak

HAWKIN'S HAUNTS

Distance: 2 mi. flat; 3.6 mi. 61 ft.; 5.3 mi. 347 ft.

Start/finish: Acorn Park, at W.15th and Buck st.
Walk downhill on Buck st.
R on bike path. Under the
first bridge. Cross Oak Patch st.
then after the apartments,
R on small path through meadow,
L around apartments.
R onto Wilson Court.

Cross W.18th Av. Up Hawkins st.

For 2 mi. **R** on 18th **R** on Quaker st. **R** on 17th.
L on Brittany. **R** on 16th. **L** on Buck to Acorn Park.

R across Hawkins onto So. Lambert.
R after ½ block to Mulkey Cemetery.
   Find Hawkins family plot.
Return to street.
Go **R**, onto Greiner. St.
R on Chaucer.
R on W. 25th Av.

For 3.6 mi., **R** on Brittany to W.18th.
Then follow directions from ✳.

L on Brittany, ½ block.
 At Bus sign, **L** on path.

When you cross the 4th street,
look right for path by 2893.
Path ends at Brighton and Timberline.

L on Timberline. **R** on Wilshire.
L at 3727-3779 sign
Straight on to path.
R at street, Blackburn.
　　　　R on Kevington. **L** on Brittany. *
　　　　Cross W. 18th. **L** ½ block.

R on Quaker st. **R** on W. 17th.
L on Brittany. **R** on W. 16th.
L on Buck st. to Acorn Park.

18

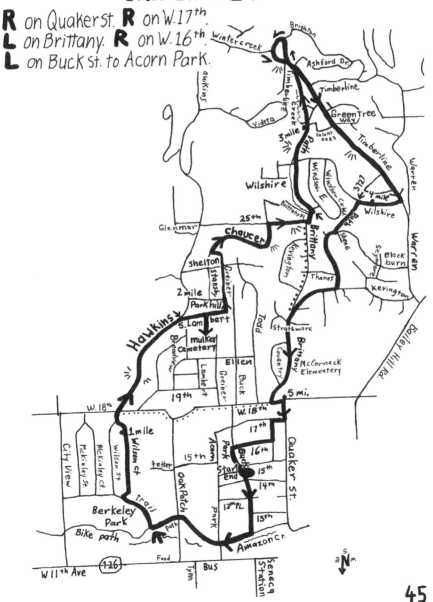

45

UO CAMPUS BIG TREES

Distance: 1.5 to 3 mi. Dots ••• show short cuts.
Start/finish: Agate St. and 13th Ave.

On Agate St. go north, past the Jaqua building.
Cross Franklin Blvd. ① red oaks
L on path after bridge over canal.
Walk along canal. Cross road. ②
L to cross Franklin Blvd. incense cedar

Deady Hall

R at end of courtyard. ③ Dawn Redwood
L at Cascade Fountain. Up steps.
R at street, pass Friendly Hall.
R around Pioneer statute.

L after Lawrence Hall sign.
L at Villard Hall.
R around next building, Deady. ④ Maple
At front, go down tree-lined
sidewalk. ⑤ firs
L at street. **L** on 13th Ave.

$$E_1' = \frac{M_2}{(M_1 + M_2)} E_0$$

R after Condon Hall. ⑥ Oaks
R at end, jog **L** thru courtyard.
L at street, **L** around to gravel
path behind Knight Library. ⑧ Holly
⑦ Pine
R at cemetery. **L** into cemetery. **R** on first road.
Circle **L** through cemetery.
R on road, jog **L** between buildings.
R on path. ⑨ Laurel ⑩ Beech ⑪ Walnut ⑫ Cork oak

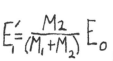

46

Cross street. Veer **R** across lawn.
L on 15th Av. Cross 15th and Agate at corner.
R into Ntrl. Hist. Museum garden.
Return to Agate, go **R** to 13th Ave.

19

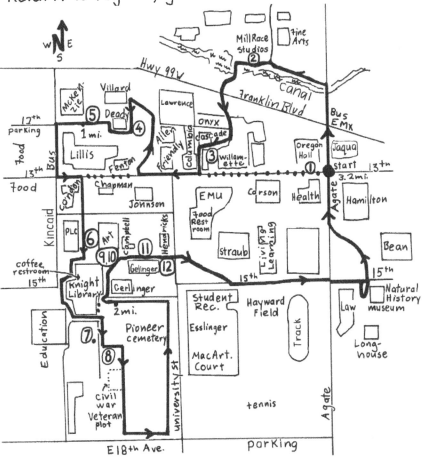

Big Trees on Campus

1. Red Oaks along 13th.
2. Incense Cedar on Right.
3. Dawn Redwood in corner.
4. Big Leaf Maple.
5. Douglas firs line path.
6. English Oaks line path.
7. Ponderosa Pine.
8. Holly Trees.
9. California Laurel.
10. European Beech.
11. Black Walnut.
12. Cork Oak: Touch!

RIBBON TRAIL Hendricks Park

Distance: 2.7 miles, very hilly
Start/finish: parking lot at Fairmount Blvd.
and Floral Hill Drive.

Cross Fairmount Blvd. to path.
R past the stone restrooms.
L at stone fountain to the
Ribbon Trail.
R on Ribbon Trail for .5 mile.
R to Laurelwood golf course,
on the trail.

At Central Dr., straight to
Laurelwood golf course.
Emerge on Central Dr.
Cross E. 27th Ave.
R on E. 26th
L on Woodland Ave.

L on Spring Blvd.
R up Fairmount Blvd.
L to trail, opposite 2800 address.

Coburg Hills

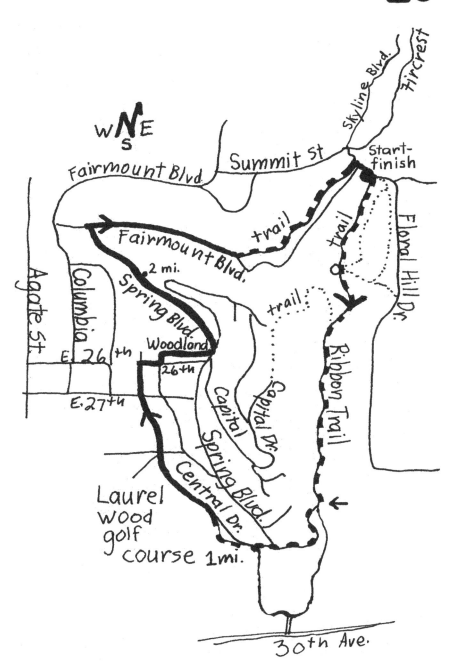

49

FIRE BREAK ROAD

→ in Hendricks Park

Distance: 2.5 miles. Moderate hills.
Start/finish: parking lot at Fairmount Ave.
and Floral Hill Drive

Cross Fairmount Ave. to path.
R past stone restrooms.
L at stone fountain,
to Ribbon Trail.
L at fork to Old Fire Break
Trail. Trail loops left.
Take all left forks, back
to the stone fountain.

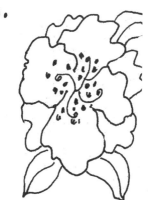

L to the Ribbon Trail, again.
Follow sian to Floral Hill Dr.
L on road, Floral Hill Dr.
L on Sylvan St.

<u>After</u> Hendricks Park sign,

Jog **R** on <u>first</u> small path, then **L** on path.
Pass picnic shelter, **L** across street.
Loop <u>up</u> on main path through park.
Straight into parking lot, then
Veer **L** to Skyline Blvd.

Straight to Prospect Dr.
Loop back to Skyline Blvd.
Return to Hendricks Park.

50

21

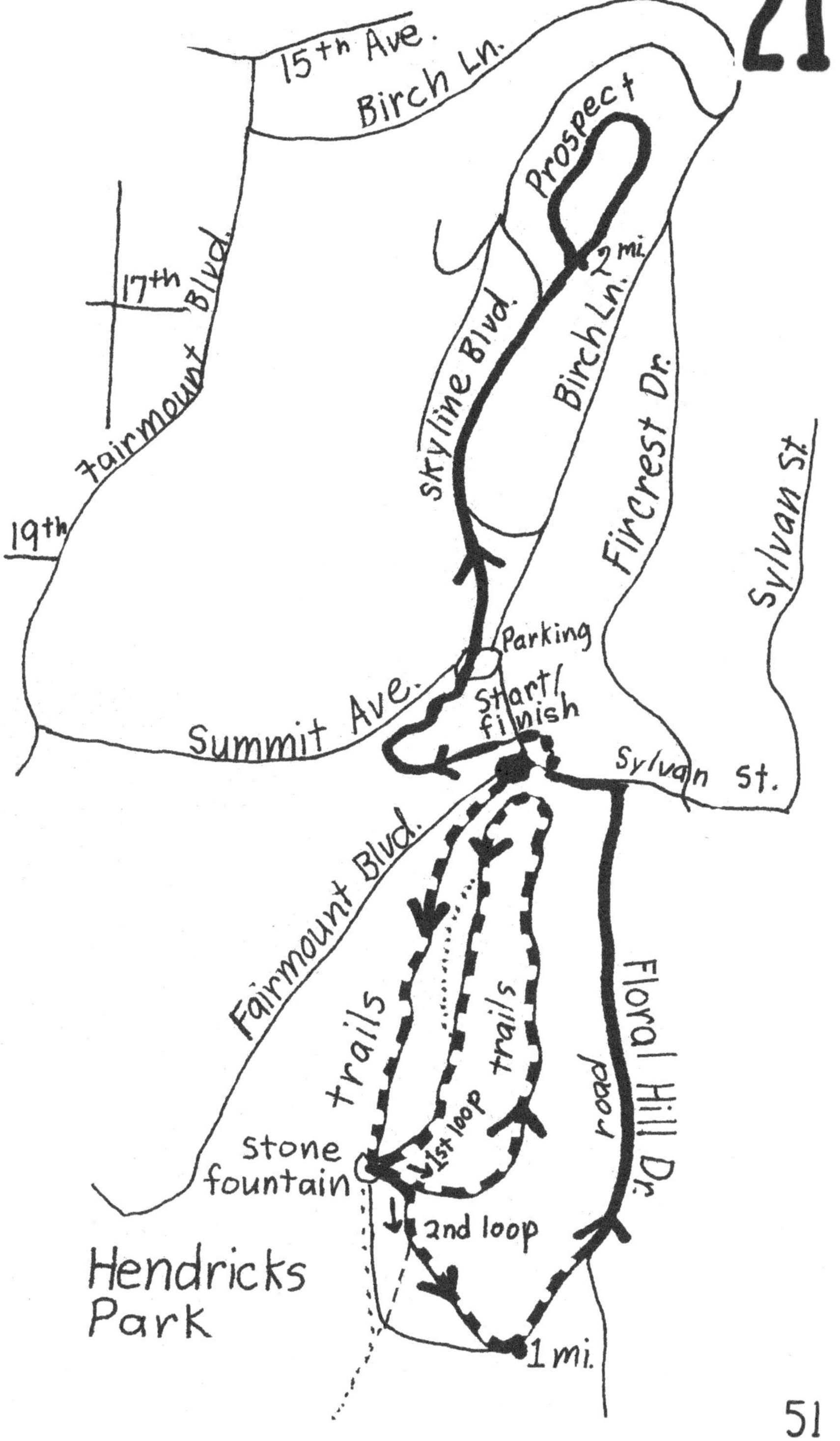

15th Ave.

Birch Ln.

Prospect

.2 mi.

Birch Ln.

17th

Fairmount Blvd.

Fircrest Dr.

Sylvan St.

Skyline Blvd.

19th

Parking

Start/finish

Summit Ave.

Sylvan St.

Fairmount Blvd.

trails

Floral Hill Dr.

road

1st loop trails

Stone fountain

2nd loop

Hendricks Park

1 mi.

FLORAL HILL

Start/finish at Hendricks Park

Distance: 3.8 miles, hilly.
Start/finish: parking lot at Fairmount Ave. and Floral Hill Drive.

Cross Fairmount Ave. to path
Go **R**, pass the stone restrooms.
L at stone fountain,
   to the Ribbon Trail.
Straight to Floral Hill Drive.
R on street, Floral Hill Drive.

Curves onto Riverview St.
R on E. 26th Ave.
Jog **R** then **L** into park.
R at the street, on left side.

L on Brackenfern Rd.
L on Laurel Hill Rd.
L down Chandler Ave.
L at end, on Moon Mountain Dr.
R through Laurel Hill Park.

22

L on E. 26th Ave.
R on end, on Riverview St.
L on Sylvan Street.

At the end, jog **R**, then **L**
to stay on Sylvan, to Hendricks Park.

yellow submarine
on E. 26th.

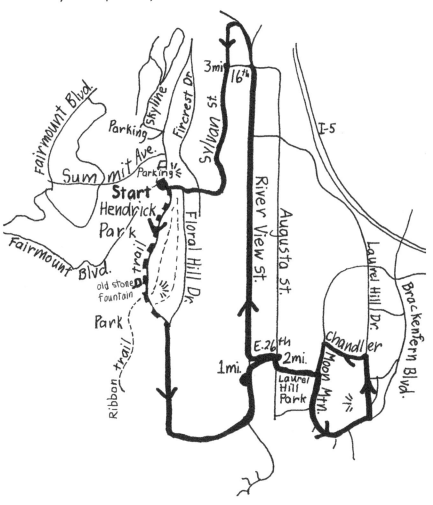

RIDGELINE TRAIL

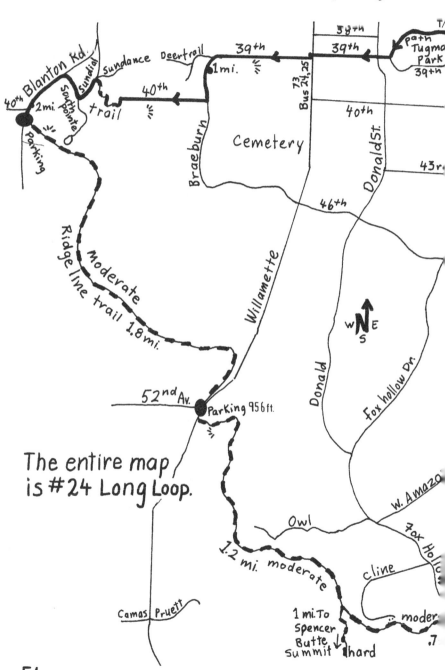

RIDGELINE TRAIL

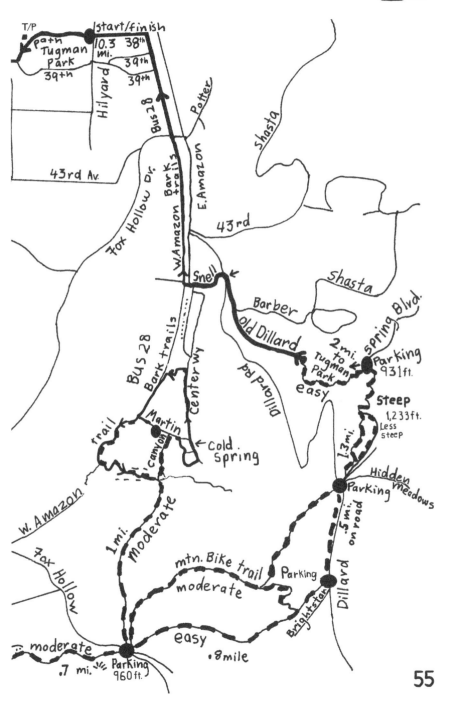

23

RIDGELINE TRAIL

Distance: 1.6 mi. to 10.3 mi. loop. Many options. Stay on the main trail.

Easy: • From Fox Hollow parking lot, walk to Dillard St. on the upper trail.

Moderate: 1. From Martin St. Trailhead, up to Fox Hollow and back, 2 mi.
2. Between Fox Hollow and Willamette.
3. From 52nd and Willamette St, walk either direction on trail.

Hard: 1. From Dillard St. over Mt. Baldy. to Spring Blvd.
2. Up Spencer Butte to summit.
3. Long Loop, below.

RIDGELINE TRAIL 24
LONG LOOP

Distance: 10.3 miles. _Hilly._ See Maps p.54-55.

Start/finish: Tugman Park, 38th and Hilyard St.
L past playground, uphill path.
R at street 39th. Cross Willamette.
jog **L** then **R** to continue up 39thAv.

Curves to Brae Burn. **R** on 40th, to trail.
L after trail, Sundance. **R** on So. Pointe.
L on Blanton to trailhead. (2 mi. mark)

Follow Ridgeline Trail to Spring Blvd.
At the trail sign,
L down trail at Spring Blvd. to Dillard.
L on Snell St.
Cross E. Amazon Pky.
R on W. Amazon Wy. on bark path.
L on 38th Av. to Tugman Park.

25 COLD SPRING

Distance: 1.5 miles, roly-poly hills
Start/finish: Martin St. Ridgeline trailhead.
Park on Martin st.

On Martin street, walk up past the kiosk,
away from the small park.(Kinney)
R on Cold Spring. **R** on Overbrook.
L at end, on Center Street.
L at 4990-5010 to the path
  between the houses.
L on the trail, immediate
R across the bridge.
L on the trail.

  At the trail end, STRAIGHT
  past the gate to the
  West Amazon Access Trail.
L at the end.
L at first trail to return
  to Martin Street.

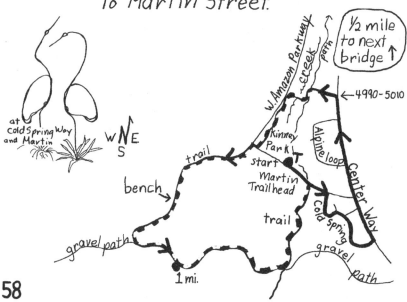

SPENCER BUTTE 26

- from Spencer Butte Park on So. Willamette St.

  Elevation: 790 ft.
  1 mile round trip.

- From S. Willamette St. and 52nd Av.
  Elevation: 1,109 ft.
  4.4 miles round trip

- From Fox Hollow at Christensen St.
  Elevation: 1,105 ft.
  3.4 miles round trip.

RIDGELINE TRAIL

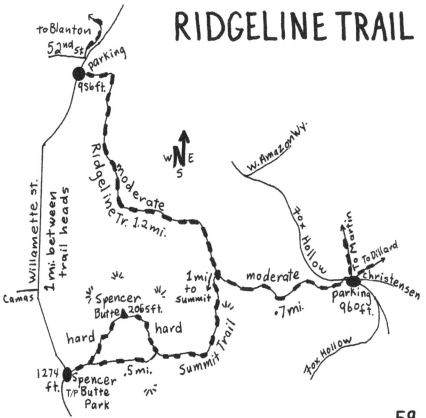

to Blanton
52nd St
parking
956 ft.

Willamette st.
1 mi: between trail heads
Camas

Ridgeline Tr. 1.2mi.

moderate

W N E S

W. Amazon Wy.

Fox Hollow

to Martin
To To Dillard
Christensen
parking
960 ft.

1 mi to summit

moderate

.7 mi.

Spencer Butte 2065ft.

hard   hard

Summit Trail

1274 ft.
T/P Spencer Butte Park

.5 mi.

Fox Hollow

BEAUTIFUL ALLEY

Distance: 1.7 mi, or 3 mi, Elevation gain: 110 ft.

Start/finish: 24th Av. and Amazon Parkway parking lot.

R from parking lot, on 24th Av.
L on Portland St.
R on 25th Av.
R on Olive St.
R on 24th Av. one block.
L on McMillan.

L up hill, Grandview. St.
L on Olive St.

> for 1.7 mi. **R** on Olive St.
> **R** on 19th Av. **R** on bike path
> before high school.

R on 23rd. Av.
R on Monroe St.
L on 21st Av. for half a block.
R into the alley.
R at end of alley, on 20th Av.

L on Washington St.
R on 19th Av.
R on bike path before school.

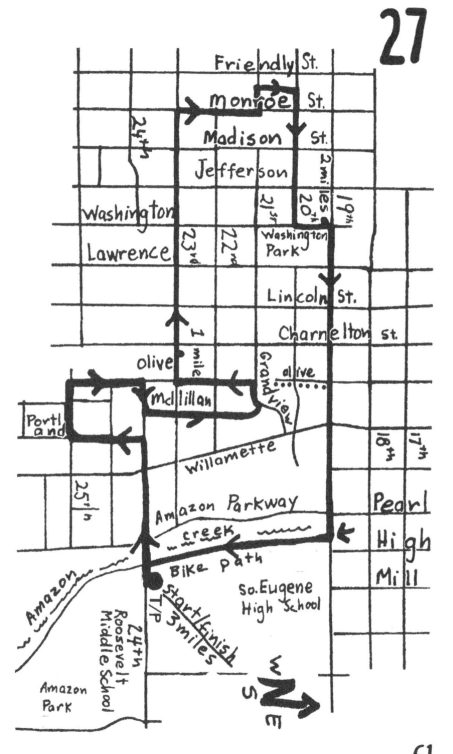

CITY VIEWS

Distances: 2.3, 3.6, 7.7, or 9.8 miles. Elev. 709 ft.
(For 7.7 mi. start at *Monroe* and *W. 27th Av.*)
(From 20th **R** on Monroe to finish.)

<u>Start/finish</u>: Amazon and 24th. **R** on 24th.
R on McMillan St. **L** up 22nd. **L** on Monroe st.

for 2.3 mi.
R on Monroe.
See * below.

R on 27th one block. **L** on Friendly St.
Cross 28th, go **R**. **L** on Adams st.
R on Tiara. **L** on Mclean Blvd.

for 3.6 mi. *
R on 26th
R on Van Buren

L at 2010-2070 Mclean. Up steps.
L at top, walk the *Loop*. Return.

L at first corner, opposite steps.
R on Blacktail. **R** at first corner, to Lasater.
L on Randy. **R** at first corner, to Ridgemont.
L on 29th. **R** on Blacktail. **R** on Herald st.

R on Blacktail. **L** at first corner, Mystic.
L on Hawkins. **R** on Wintercreek st.
L on Timberline Dr.

At Brighton St. corner, **R** down path.
Cross 4 streets, look **R** for path.
R at end, Brittany St.
At end, cross 18th. **L** one block.
R on Quaker st. **R** on bike path.
R over foot bridge, opposite school.

L just after bridge onto bark trail.
L after houses to street, 20th

(for 7.7 mi, **R** on Monroe St.)
* (2.3 and 3.6 mi., **R** on 20th.)

28

L on Madison St. after path, one block.
R on 19th. **R** on path before high school.

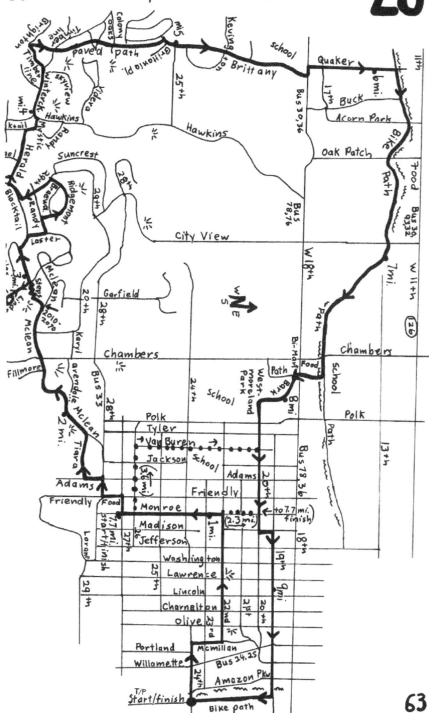

EDGEWOOD TRAILS I

Distance: 6.4 miles. Elevation gain, 500 ft.

Start/Finish: Amazon Pkwy. and 24th Av.

R on 24th Av. **L** on Portland St.
R on 26th Av. **L** on McMillan St.
Down stairs. Past stores.
Cross 29th Av. at light. **L** on 29th Av.

R on Portland St. **R** on 30th Av.
Up steps to trail. Take uphill trails
to picnic shelter. Pass the house.
Cross Crest st. go **L**.

R on Olive St. **L** on 35th Av.
R **R** on Willamette St.
R into cemetery. **R** on road to top.
Exit **R** to street, 40th Av.
L on Brae Burn.
R on Normandy Way, 25 yards.

L on Nature Trail. When path crosses
street, look right for next path.
Take left forks, continue downhill
to end of public path.

L on Brookside Dr. **R** on Brae Burn.
Cross Willamette St. to 46th Av.

L on Pearl St. Straight to 41st Av.
L on Donald St.
R on 39th Av. Cross street.
L on path to Tugman Park. (restrooms)

L at first fork in park.
L over bridge between houses.
R on street, 36th **L** at first corner,
R on 31st Av. **L** on bike path.

29

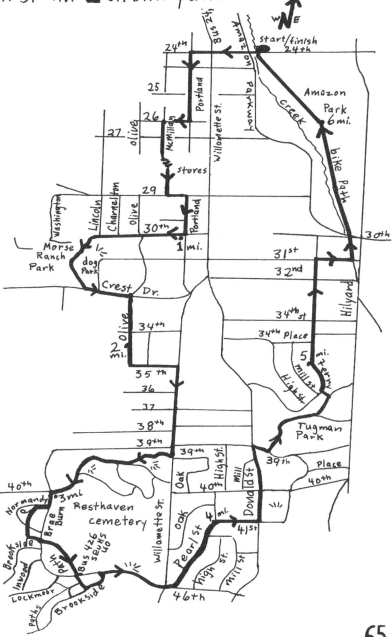

EMERALD HILL

Distance: 1.5 mi. from 24thAv. at University St.
2.5 mi. from 24thAv. at Amazon Pkwy.
Elevation: 116 ft.

Start/finish: Amazon Pkwy and 24thAv.

L on 24thAv.
L on Alder, one block.
R on 23rd Av.

    R on Emerald St.
    R on 28thAv.
    R on Elinor St. into cemetery.

   R on path to top of hill.
     • Take time to explore the cemetery.
     • Face the front of the big mausoleum.
go **L** down longer road.

> For 1.5 mi. option, straight on Street,
> Potter St., to park.

L on 25thAv.
R on Alder, one block.
L on 24th Av.

mason
symbol
on a
tombstone

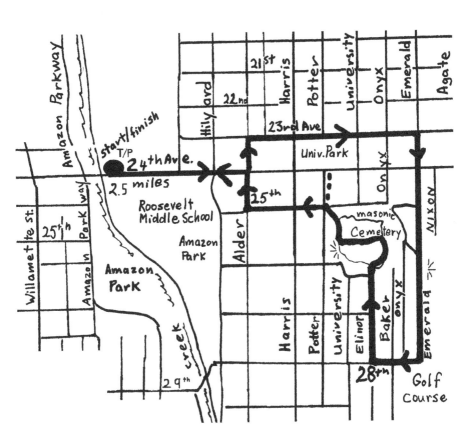

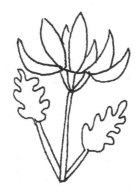

30

ELK STREET

Distance: 4.5 miles. easy
Start/finish: 24th Ave. and Amazon Pkwy.

L on 24th Ave. **L** on Alder St.
R on 23rd. Ave.
L on Columbia St. cross the
old trolley tracks,
Straight up to 22nd Ave.

L on Fairmount Blvd.
R on McMorran St.
L at the corner.
R on Fairmount Blvd.

R on Elk St. **L** at corner.
Pass through to street.
Cross Summit St.
L down Summit St.

R on Fairmount Blvd.
L on E. 15th Ave.
L on Villard St.

R on E. 19th Ave.
L on University St.
R on 24th Ave.

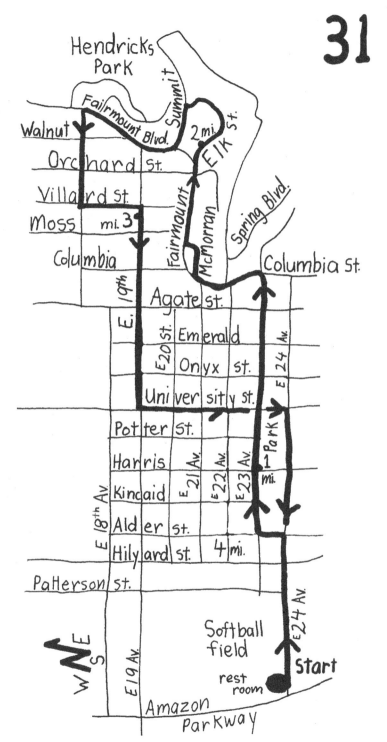

31

FAIRMOUNT TRAIL

Distance: *2 mi., flat. 2.5 mi., 4 mi. Elev. 230 ft.

Start/finish: Amazon Pky. and 24th Av.
[For 2.5 mi. start at University and 24th]

From the parking lot:

L on 24th Av. **L** on Alder St.
R on 23rd Av.

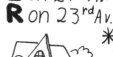

* [For 2 mi. option, **L** on Agate St.
L on 21st Av. **L** on Alder St.
R on 24th Av.]

L on Columbia St.
R up Fairmount Blvd.
L at fork, to Hendricks Park.

L down trail opposite #2800,
where the curb ends.
When the trail ends at the
road, **L** on path.
Pass the drinking fountain,
Cross the road, Summit Av.

L down path along Summit Av.
L on Fairmount Blvd.
R on 21st Av. **L** on Alder St.
R on 24th Av.

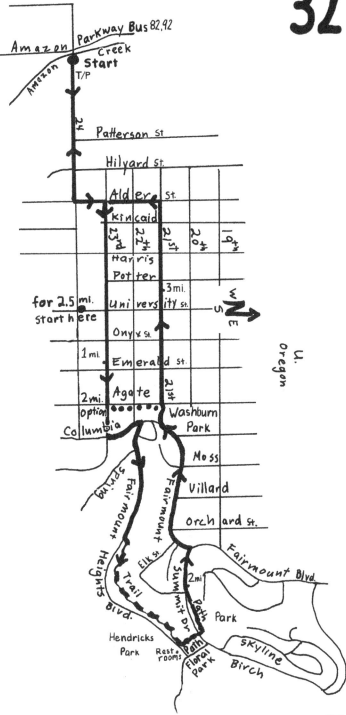

32

FOUR CREEKS

Distances: 2 mi. flat. or 7 mi., hilly.
Elevation: 540 ft. for 7 miles.

Start/finish: Amazon Pkwy. and 24th Av.
R on 24th Av. **L** on Portland St.
R on 26th Av. **L** on McMillan St.
Down steps. Past stores.
Cross 29th Av. at light. **L** on 29th

For 2 mi. option, straight on 29th Av.
L on paved path to finish.

R on Portland St.
R on 30th Av. Up steps to trail.
Take uphill paths to picnic
shelter. Pass the house, to street.

Cross street, Crest Dr. Go **R**.
Curves **L** onto storey Blvd.
When the sidewalk ends,
continue straight on to
Blanton Road, curve **R** at top of hill.

L on Sandpointe Dr.
Do the loop to the end.
Return to go **R** on Sundance St.
R on Sundial Rd. Pass guardrail.
L down trail. Through trees.
Emerge on 40th Av.

33

Cross Brae Burn Dr.
Go into cemetery.
L on cemetery road, downhill.
Cross Willamette St. go **L**. **R** on 39th Av.

Cross Donald st. **L** on path to park.
L at street, Hilyard st.
Cross 30th Av. (at 31st)
L to paved path to 24th Av.

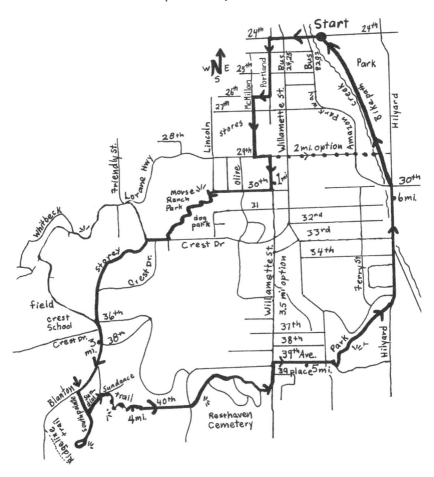

MANSIONS and MEADOW

Distance: 4.4 mi., 7 mi. or 9 mi. All hilly!
Elevation gain: 834 ft.

Start/finish: Amazon Pkwy. and 24th Av.
L on 24th Av. **L** on Alder St.
R on 23rd Av. **L** on Columbia St.
R up Fairmount Blvd. **L** at fork.

Just before next street (Floral Hill)
R on the path along stone restrooms.
Straight past old stone fountain.
L at first fork in trail, on to Capital Bl.
Sharp turn **L** on Spring Blvd.

For 4.4 mi. option, **R** on 27th Av.
R on Columbia St. **L** on 24th Av.

R on Central. Jog **R** then **L** to trail.
to 30th Av. Cross bridge, over 30th.

R on Fir land st.

For 7 mi., **R** on Agate
L on 31st **R** on 32nd.
R on Alder. **L** on 24th

L on Agate St.
L to Spring Blvd. at So. Shasta Loop sign.

At the trail sign. **R** down trail.
Emerge on Old Dillard Rd.
L on Snell St.
R on E. Amazon Dr.
R on 39th to Kincaid St.
L At 35th Av., **R** on Alder st.
L on 24th Av., back to finish.

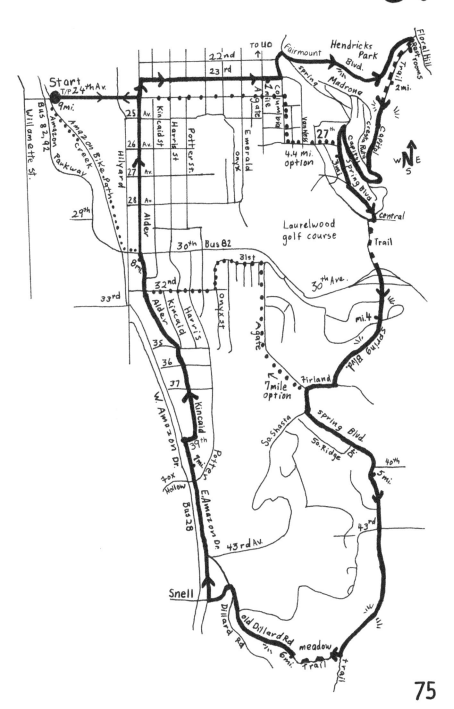

34

LAFFERTY PARK

Distance: 5.5 miles.
Start/finish: 24th and Amazon Parkway.

R on 24th, across Amazon Pkwy.
L along Amazon Parkway.
R on 26th, 1 block.
L on Oak st., at end, jog **L** then
R on Pearl St. to end.
L at end, to path. **R** on street.
curves into 30th Ave.

L on Willamette St. to light.
R across Willamette st.
L along sidewalk. Before the
next light, **R** past the
barrier onto Portland st.

L on 31st, Into W. Morse Park.
R at first fork. **L** after bridge.
Take paths going uphill.
Pass Wayne Morse home.

Cross Crest Dr., into Park.
L on Street, Mary Ln.
Curves up to Fulvue Dr.

L after 350 Fulvue, into driveway.
R on path, to Horizon.
R on Crest Dr. **R** on Fulvue.

R on Mary Ln. into Cemetery.
Veer **L**. **R** onto lowest road.
Pass the chain gate, down the
gravel road. Straight at street.

35

L on Willamette St. to light.
R across street, **R** to 33rd.
L on 33rd. **L** on Hilyard St.
R at crosswalk to 32nd.
L on Alder St. **L** on 24th.

path
start/finish
Parking   24th Av.
E.24th   Roosevelt
                          Middle
24th   School
25th   5 mi.
26th   Park   Kincaid St.
                 Oak
27th   Amazon Pkwy.   Bike Path
                 Willamette St.
28th   28th
Jefferson   Market of
                 choice
                 W. 29th   Oak st.   Pearl   Highst.   Mill st.   Ferry st.   Hilyard St.
Lincoln st.
                 W. 30th
                 W. 31st   30th   1mi.
Wayne   trail   31st Av.   32 nd
Morse   32nd Av.
Park   Olive st.   Prall Dr.   Portland
2 mi.   Crest   33rd. Av.
         Calvary   E. Amazon Dr.
Lafferty Cemetery Donald st.
Park   34th   34th 4 mi.
Crest Dr. Mary Ln.
         Fulvue 2nd
Horizon   path   Olive   Willamette St.
st.   1st time

ADIDAS-REXIUS TRAILS

Start/finish: 24th Av. and Amazon Parkway
Distance: 5.5 miles, flat, mostly bark trails

From the parking lot,
cross 24th Av.
Jog **R** then **L** on to bark.
R at every fork.

At end, straight on paved path.
Cross the first street, and
go straight onto foot path.
L at end, on E. 33rd. Ave.
Cross Hilyard st.
R across E. Amazon Dr.
L on bark trail along
   W. Amazon Dr.

At the end, curve **L** on bark,
back to Hilyard st. and 33rd.

R across E. Amazon Dr.
L across Hilyard st.
R on small footpath you
   were on before.

Straight on paved path,
and onto the bark trail.

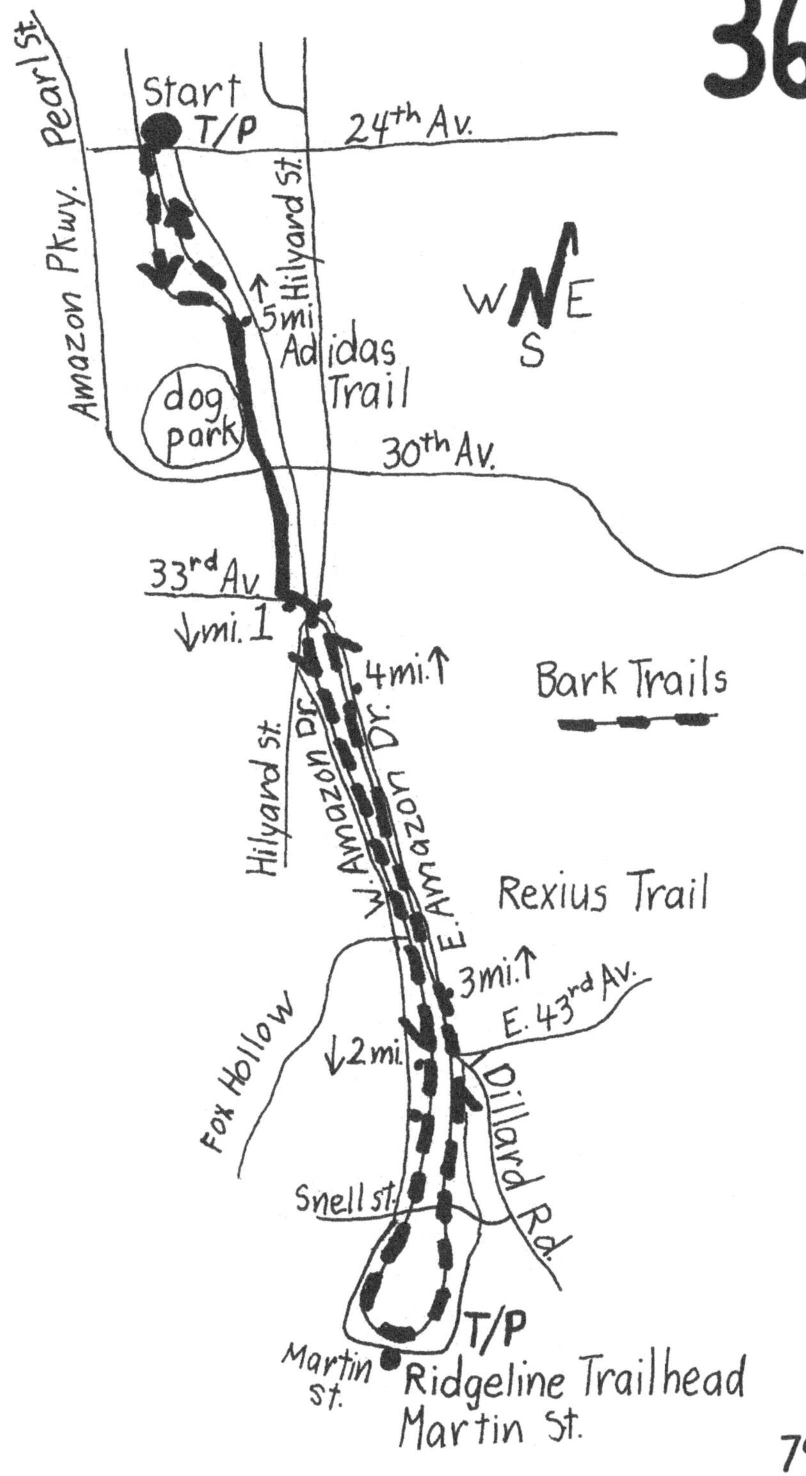

36

Pearl St.

Amazon Pkwy.

Start T/P

24th Av.

Hilyard St.

5mi Adidas Trail

W **N** E
S

dog park

30th Av.

33rd Av
↓mi. 1

Bark Trails

Hilyard st.

W. Amazon Dr.

E. Amazon Dr.

4mi.↑

Rexius Trail

3mi.↑

E. 43rd Av.

↓2.mi.

Fox Hollow

Dillard Rd.

Snell st.

T/P
Martin st.
Ridgeline Trailhead
Martin St.

EDGEWOOD EXPLORING

Distance: 1 mile with optional paths.
Elevation: 108 ft.

Start/finish: Brae Burn Dr. and W. 40th Av.
Walk downhill. **R** on Normandy Way
After 25 yards, **L** on Nature Trail,
between houses 4031 and 4047.
When you cross the street
look right for the path.

Cross the bridge. **R** for easy
1/4 mile loop. Return to bridge.
Continue down path.

At the next bridge: 3 options.
R across the bridge to a
three way intersection.

Here: **1.R** goes to Lockmoor Dr.
2.L goes up the valley,
becomes very steep,
emerging on Brookside Dr.
L on Brookside Dr.
L on BraeBurn Dr. to W. 40th Av.

3. L Before the bridge.
L at next corner, Brookside Dr.
L at corner, Brae Burn Dr., to finish.

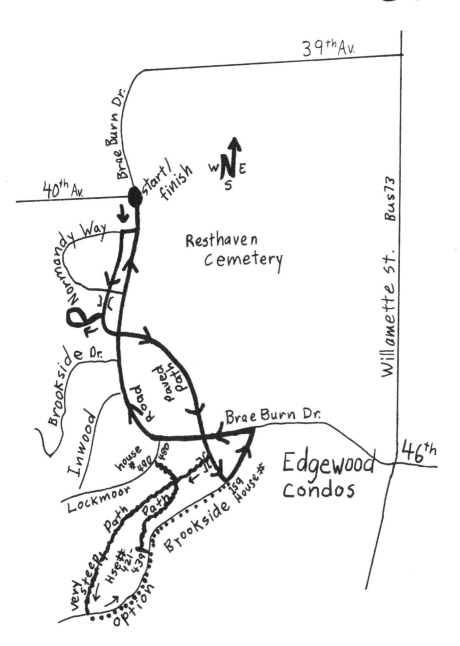

37

39th Av.

Brae Burn Dr.

40th Av.

Normandy Way

Start/finish

W N E S

Resthaven Cemetery

Brookside Dr.

Inwood

Lockmoor

Road

Paved Path

Brae Burn Dr.

house #490

490

Path

very steep Path

Hse #421-439

option

Brookside House #159

Edgewood Condos

Willamette St.   Bus 73

46th

EDGEWOOD TRAILS II

Distance: 2.4 miles. Elevation: 222 ft.

Start/finish: Donald St. and E. 40th Av.

On 40th Av., face Edgewood Center, go **R.**
R on Oak St. **L** on Pearl St.
L on 39th Av.
Cross Willamette St.
Enter the cemetery.
R on road to top.
<u>Before</u> the downhill,
Exit right to street, 40th Av.

L on Brae Burn Dr.
R on Normandy Way, 25 yards.
between houses 4031 and 4047.

L on to Nature Trail. At the
first street, look **R** for trail.
Cross the bridge.
R for short loop through trees.
Return to bridge. **C**ontinue downhill.
L at every fork, go downhill.

38

Through Edgewood condos on path.
R on Brae Burn Dr.
Cross Willamette St. to 46th Av.
L on Pearl St. **R** on 41st St.
L on Donald St. to 40th Av. to finish.

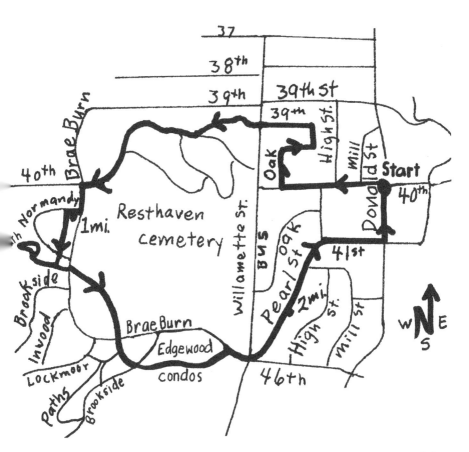

LCC Labrynith and Trails

Distance: 2.7 miles.
Start/finish: Building 1

Face Bldg. 1 entrance. **L** on sidewalk.
R in to garden. **L** at fountain to
walk the labrynith.
Return to the sidewalk. Go **R.**

R at the end. **L** on bark trail.
Stay on the trail, down around
the soccer fields.
Cross the road, to a faint path.
R at the end, into the woods.

R at the street, Eastway Dr.
L on E. Schaffer Dr.

or straight across street
on to bark path, back to Bldg. 1

R at end. **L** on to gravel road, Go **R.**
At next road, **R** down to parking lot.
L opposite Lot E.

L around buildings to
The Learning Garden.
Explore.
Return to Lot E.
Continue around Bldg. 19.
Pass Bldg. 17. **L** at end.

Poison Oak

39

R at doors to "The Center."
Circle **L** around "The Center."
to Bldg. 11 Down the stairs.
Jog **R** then **L.** Straight to Bldg. 1.

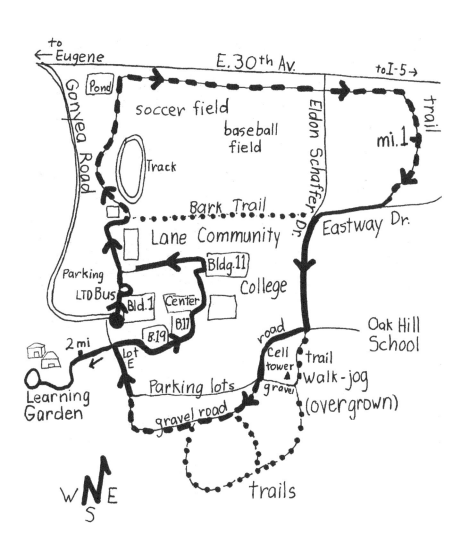

BY-GULLY PATH

Distance: 5.25 miles, flat
Start/finish: Island Park, Springfield

Take paved path along the river.
Cross the first street, W. D st.
Straight onto Kelly Blvd.

Birding site

R on Fairview Dr.
L at Mill st, before 1st st.
  onto By-Gully Path, veer **L.**

L at end, on street, Quinalt Ave.
R on Linden Av.
R on Tamarak st.
At end, Cottonwood Av. jog **R**,
then **L** across Menlo Park.
L on street, Sequonia Av.
R on Aspen st.

R on Windsor Ct. **R** on Wimbledon.
R on sidewalk between #1479 and #1463.
R on Windsor. Ct. **R** on Aspen st.

L on path along river.
R on street, W. D st.
R on path, opposite Kelly Blvd.

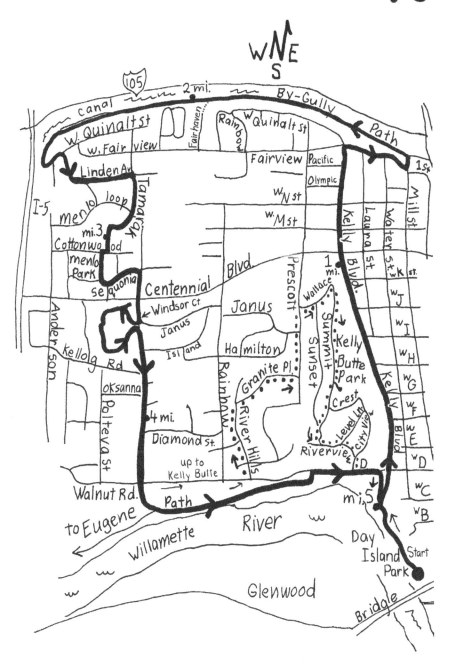

40

KELLY BUTTE

Distance: 2 mi. flat or 3.5 mi. Elev. 180 ft.

Start/finish: So. "A" St. and Pioneer Pkwy. in parking lot behind Chamber of Commerce, the old depot.

Walk through the arbor at the end of the parking lot. **L** after arbor, **R** on path. Through the parking lot to Day Island Park.

view of Sisters Peaks

Stay on path along river. Curves **R** over footbridge.
L at street, "D" St.
L on to bike path.
R at fork in path.
R on road Aspen St, one block. Cross street, "D" st. Go **R**.

For 2mi, straight on "D" st. **R** on Water St.

L on River Hills. **R** on Granite Pl.
L on Prescott Ln. **R** on Wallace Ln.
Curves **R** on to Summit Blvd.

Sharp **L** into Kelly Butte Park.
L around loop. Pause for view.
Return to Summit Blvd. Go **L**.

Cross "D" St. Go **L** on "D" St.
R on Water St. on to path
over footbridge.
Immediate **L** on path.
Under the bridge, back to start.

41

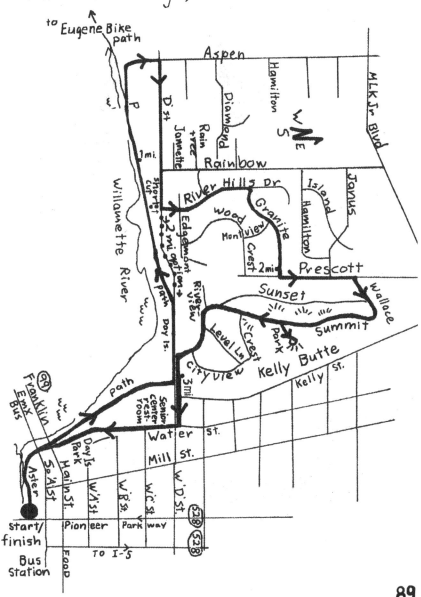

WASHBURNE DISTRICT

Distance: 1.2 mi., 2.3 mi., or 3.5 mi. Flat.

Start/finish: So. 'A' St. at Pioneer Pkwy. Park behind Spr. Chamber of Commerce.

Cross So. 2nd St. Go **L** on to Pioneer Parkway W.

R on 'A' St. **L** on 10th St one block.
L on 'B' St.

For 1.2 mi., **L** on 4th St.
R on Main. **L** on Pioneer.

R on 4th St., one block. **R** on 'C' St.
L on 10th St., one block. **L** on 'D' St.

For 2.3 mi., **L** on 4th St. **R** on Main St.
L on Pioneer Pkwy. to end.

R on 4th St., 1 block. **R** on 'E' St.
L on 10th St., one block. **L** on 'F' St.

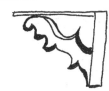

L on 4th St.
R on Main St., 2 blocks.
L on Pioneer Pkwy. W to end.

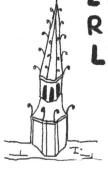

Historical information at:
→ Sprg. Chamber of Commerce
→ and online at Washburne
            Historical District.

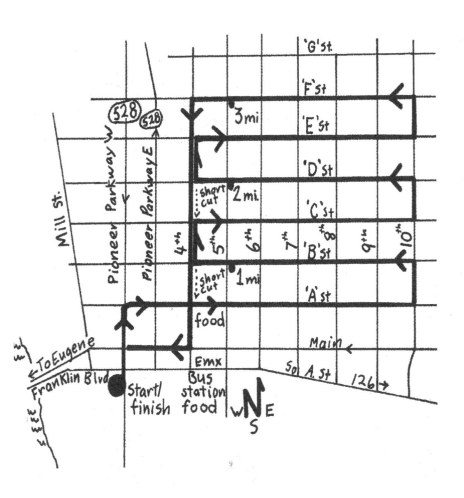

42

WILLAMITTE HEIGHTS PARK

Distance: 2 miles. Big hill.
Start/finish: S. 'A' st. and Pioneer Parkway at
    Springfield Depot and information.

On S. 'A' st. go east to S. 5th.
R on S. 5th, curves **R.**
L across railroad tracks.
Up the steps. Circle right
    through the cemetery,
L on street, S. 'C' st.
R on S. 4th. **L** on Park st.
R on S. 5th.

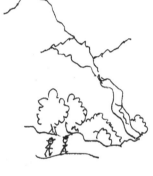

R on Union st. At corner,
straight onto trail.
L at first fork. In the park,
veer **R** to trail up to the tower.
Return to the park.

R on the road, pass the barrier,
Veer **R** down the trail, it curves.
R on the road (S. G st.)
L on S. 4th st. **L** on S. D st. one block.
R on S. 3rd. one block.
L on S. C st. **R** at end (S. 2nd st.)

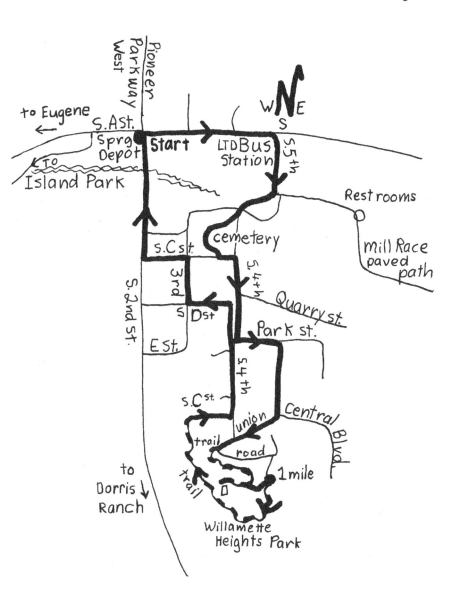

to Eugene
S. A St.
Sprg Depot
To Island Park

Start

LTD Bus Station

W N E S

S. 5th

Rest rooms

cemetery

mill Race paved path

S. C st.
3rd
S D st
S. 4th
Quarry st.

Pioneer Parkway West

S. 2nd St.

E St.

Park st.

S. 4th

S. C st.
union
trail
road
Central Blvd.

to Dorris Ranch

1 mile

trail

Willamette Heights Park

DORRIS RANCH

Distance: 1.5 to 4 miles, hill, 126 ft.
Start/finish: S.A st. at Pioneer Parkway, W.
    Springfield Depot and information.
    (or Dorris Ranch.)

East on S.A st. **R** on S.5th, curves right.
    L across railroad tracks.
Up steps, through cemetery.
R on street, (S.C) ½ block.
L on S.3rd. **R** on S.E st
L at end, on S.2nd.

In Dorris Ranch, **L** on paved
path. **L** through the Living
History Village, back to path.
Cross the paved path, down
gravel path, around the house.
Pass to the **L** of the kiosk.
Across the bridge, to the river.

The path curves **L** at the river
① **L** at first fork, through orchard.
   veer **R** through trees, **R** on road. (4 miles)
② **L** on second fork, quick **R** (#6).
   R along orchard, to small path.
   L at orchard (Goat Orchard) **L** on to dirt road.
   L on to next dirt road.
   R at end, back the start.

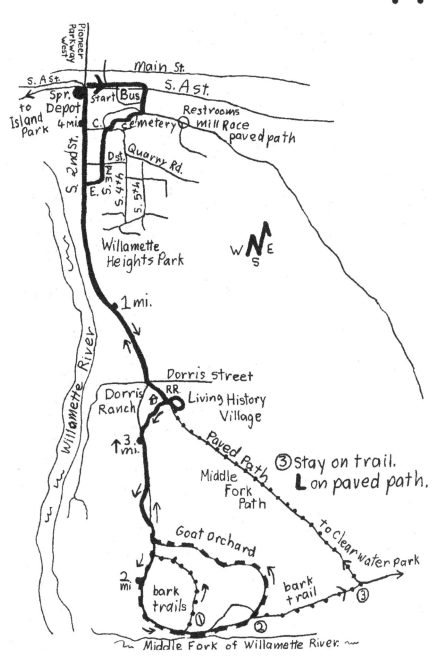

44

Pioneer Parkway West

Main St.

S. A st.   S. A st.

S. A st.

to Island Park

Spr. Depot 4 mi.

Start   Bus

Restrooms

C.   cemetery   mill Race   paved path

S. 2nd St.

D st.   Quarry Rd.

E.   S. 3rd   S. 4th   S. 5th

Willamette Heights Park

W N E
   S

1 mi.

Willamette River

Dorris street

Dorris Ranch   RR.   Living History Village

3. mi.

Paved Path

Middle Fork Path

③ stay on trail.
L on paved path.

to clearwater park

Goat Orchard

2 mi.   bark trails   bark trail

①   ②   ③

Middle Fork of Willamette River.

MILL RACE PATH to
CLEARWATER PARK
4 miles one way. Flat, paved

TRAILHEADS

Mill Race: on S.5th, **L** to Booth Kelly.
Middle Fork at Dorris Ranch.
Jasper Road at 32nd St.
Clearwater Park, off Jasper Road.

MIDDLE FORK PATH
Starts at Dorris Ranch. flat, paved
Distance: 2.5 miles to intersect with
Mill Race Path.

6.2 mile
<u>Loop option</u>: At the Mill Race Path,
  L to Booth-Kelly Trail head.
  Continue to Main Street.
  L on Main St.
  L on S. 2nd. St. (1 mi. to Dorris R.)

<u>Trail Option</u>: 2 miles, flat.
R on the bark path back
through the orchards.

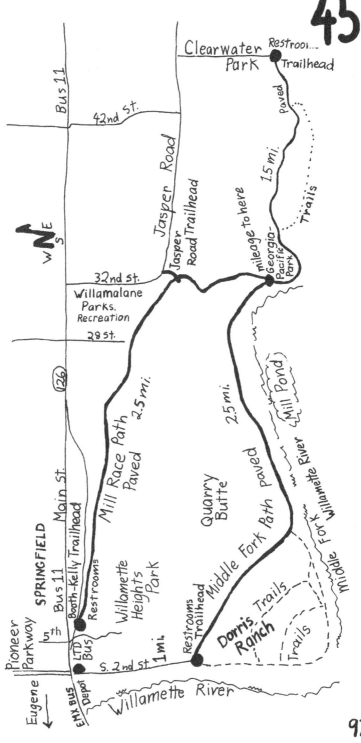

45

Clearwater Park

Restroo...
Trailhead

paved

Bus 11

42nd St.

Jasper Road

1.5 mi.

Jasper Road Trailhead

mileage to here

Trails

Jasper Road Trailhead

32nd St.

Georgia-Pacific Park

Willamalane Parks. Recreation

28 St.

126

Mill Pond

2.5 mi.

2.5 mi.

Main St.

Mill Race Path Paved

Quarry Butte

Middle Fork Path Paved

Middle Fork Willamette River

SPRINGFIELD

Bus 11

Booth-Kelly Trailhead

Willamette Heights Park

Restrooms

Pioneer Parkway

5th

Restrooms Trailhead

Dorris Ranch

Trails

Trails

Middle Fork

LTD Bus

S. 2nd St.

1 mi.

Eugene

EMX BUS Depot

Willamette River

HAYDEN BRIDGE WAY

Distance: 2.4 mi.* or 3.4 mi. Flat. (No restrooms)
Start/finish: 1514 Blackstone, off 5ᵗʰ St. and
Hayden Bridge Way.

Walk into Royal Delle Park.
Circle **L**, pass the playground
to exit the park.
R on street (Cambridge.)
R on 3rd St. **L** on Seward Av.
Straight on to Wayside.

R around the loop. **R** on Wayside Ln.
Cross the street at Hayden Bridge Way
roundabout. Go **L**.
R on Shady lane.
L on Woodlane Dr.

L on 5ᵗʰ St.   (*2.4 mi. Continue. **L** on Blackstone St.)

Quick **R** on Hayden Bridge <u>PLACE</u>.
R on 8ᵗʰ St, 1 block. **L** on V st.
L on 10ᵗʰ St. Cross Hayden Br. Way.
onto Mckenzie Crest Dr.

Curves into Mansfield st.
L on 5ᵗʰ St.
R on Blackstone. St.

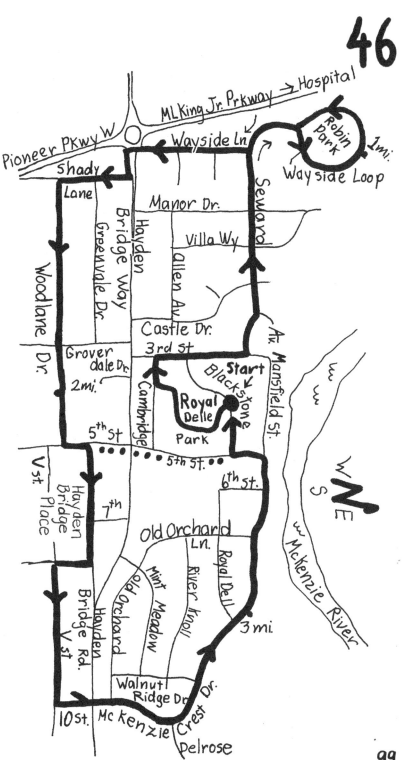

46

RIVER BEND RIVER TRAIL

Distance: 2.5 mi. flat.
Start/finish: Gamebird Park.
    at Mallard St. and Grouse St.

Walk on Grouse St.
L on Flamingo St.
L on Game Farm Rd. 1 block.
R at Mallard St. In 10 steps, **L** on paved path.

At end, take crosswalk across street. **R** along same street. Curves **R** (Martin Luther King Jr. Py) **L** on path into Riverbend Commons.

Cross street, go straight. **R** to view water feature.
Up steps, cross street.
L on sidewalk along hospital.

R at street. Straight into the Lyle Hatfield Riverside Trail.

R at fork. Stay on main path.
L on first street. Cross MLK Jr. Pky.
Straight onto Mallard St.
to Gamebird Park.

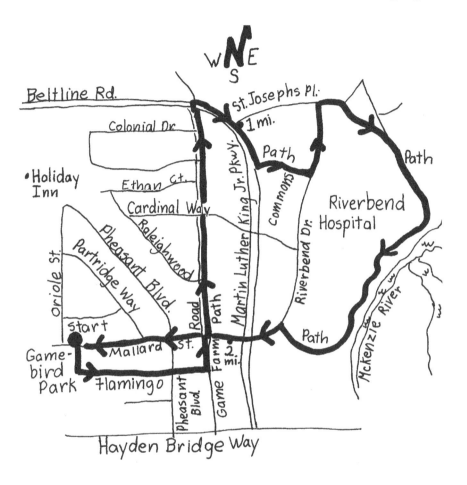

47

Beltline Rd.

W **N** E
S

St. Josephs Pl.

1 mi.

Colonial Dr.

Path

Path

• Holiday
  Inn

Ethan Ct.

Cardinal Way

Riverbend
Hospital

Commons

Raleighwood

Pheasant Blvd.

Partridge Way

Oriole St.

Martin Luther King Jr. Pkwy.

Riverbend Dr.

Mckenzie River

Start

Road

Path

Path

Game-
bird
Park

Mallard   St.

2 mi.

Flamingo

Pheasant Blvd.

Game Farm

Hayden Bridge Way

THURSTON H.S. to IVY St.

Distances: *2.8 mi. flat, or *2.1 mile, flat.
or 5 mi. 270 ft. hill. (no restrooms)

Start/finish: 60th St. and E St. Park on street
behind the tennis courts

On E st, walk east into Thurston Park.
Veer **L** to the street. **R** on street, F St.
Curves into 64th st. **L** on D st. ⌐*for 2.8 mi,
Cross 65 st, go **L**. **R** on E st. └see *R on A st.⌐

R on 67 st. **L** on B st. **L** on 68th
R on 69 st. Cross Main St, go **R**.
L on s68 st. *R** on Aster St.
⌐☆Park on s68
└and Aster⌐ **L** on s67 st.

L on Ivy St. **L** on s70 St.
R on sE st. Curve **L** onto s. 71 St.
L on Main St. (☆**L** on s68 st.
(if you parked there.)

Cross 69 st. **R** across Main St.
* **L** on A st. **R** on 64 st.
L into Thurston Park.
L through the Park on to the
bark path to Thurston High Sch.

Opposite tennis courts,
R on path to E st. and 60 st.

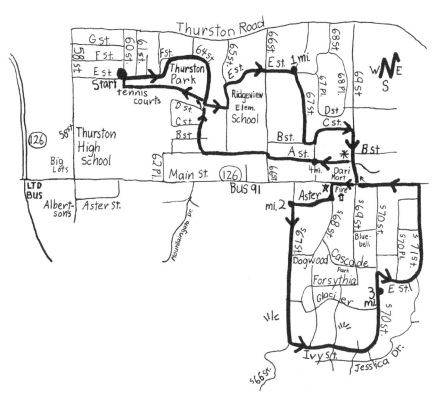

48

MOUNTAINGATE TRAIL

Distance: 4.5 miles. 400 foot elevation gain.
Start/finish: 58 st. and Aster st. for parking.

Go south (away from Main st.)
   on ^{S}58 st.
L on ^{S}57 st. Curves into ^{S}58 st.
L onto bark path before pond.
Go straight, pass the playground.
L on street, Mountaingate Dr.

L on trail between houses, 780, 746.
Straight across the foot bridge.
Up the path, into the woods.

L on street (Graystone)
between houses 6082, 6078.
L on Mountaingate Dr.
At stop sign, cross street,
R on Forest Ridge Dr.

At the end, pass the barrier.
Veer **L** to the single boulder.
Down the old road.
Cross the street, **L** on sidewalk.
R on bark path around pond.
R on the street. **R** on ^{S}58 st.

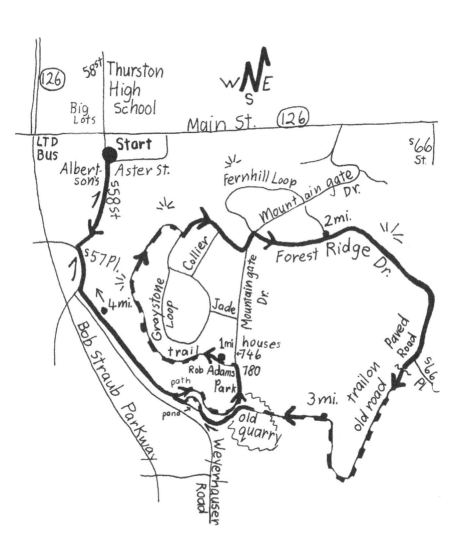

49

50 THURSTON HILLS TRAIL

Distance: *North Access Trail, 1.9 mi. one way*
Spine Trail, 1.2 mi. one way
elevation gain, 800 ft. up total

Start/finish: 7575 Main St. (126) Mckenzie Hwy.

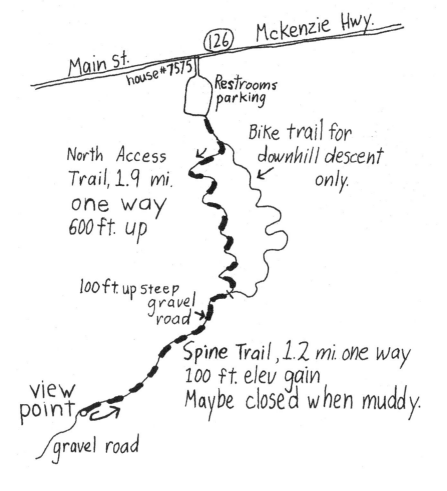

Mckenzie Hwy.

(126)

Main St.

house #7575

Restrooms
parking

Bike trail for
downhill descent
only.

North Access
Trail, 1.9 mi.
one way
600 ft. up

100 ft. up steep
gravel
road

Spine Trail, 1.2 mi. one way
100 ft. elev gain
Maybe closed when muddy.

view
point

gravel road

Diary of Walks

Route	Miles	Date

Diary of Walks

Route	Miles	Date

Diary of Walks

Route	Miles	Date

About the Author and Illustrator
Tyler E. Burgess

Born in 1950 in the shadow of the Bighorn Mtns,
I grew up on a cattle ranch near Sheridan,
Wyoming. While earning a business degree at
the University of Wyoming, I married, had two
children, Sara and Damon. We moved to
Billings, Montana, raised the children, divorced
and I eventually moved to Eugene, Oregon.

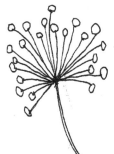

For athletics, I have always loved
outdoor sports. In my 40's I
played soccer, did triathlons,
multi-sport events and solo
backpack trips in wilderness
areas.

In 2000 I founded Walk With Me.
I taught fitness walking classes
at the University of Oregon
and Lane Community College.
For 17 years I coached marathon
walking training, and directed
four Walk-With-Me marathons.

For 15 years I gave 34 walking
tours in 10 different countries,
for over 150 people, doing all
the organizing and guiding.

Currently, I walk, cycle and sketch the world.

110

Made in the USA
Middletown, DE
04 June 2024

55183875R00066